THE BOURGEOIS MIND

THE BOURGEOIS MIND
and other essays

by
NICHOLAS BERDYAEV

Essay Index Reprint Series

BOOKS FOR LIBRARIES PRESS, INC.
FREEPORT, NEW YORK

PUBLISHER'S NOTE

We have to thank the Editors of the *Dublin Review*, *Christendom*, and the *Hibbert Journal* for permission to include essays taken in whole or in part from these journals. All these have been revised for publication in book form. *The Bourgeois Mind* and *Man and Machine* are translated from the Russian by Countess Bennigsen; the other two essays are from the French. The whole collection has been revised by Donald Attwater, who also translated the last essay.

First published 1934
Reprinted 1966

CONTENTS

I

THE BOURGEOIS MIND

THE BOURGEOIS MIND

WHAT does the word *bourgeois* actually mean? It has remained unexplained, though it has been so much used and so often misapplied. Even when superficially used it is a word with a magic power of its own, and its depth has to be fathomed. The word designates a spiritual state, a direction of the soul, a peculiar consciousness of being. It is neither a social nor an economic condition, yet it is something more than a psychological and ethical one—it is spiritual, ontological. In the very depths of his being, or non-being, the bourgeois is distinguishable from the not-bourgeois; he is a man of a particular spirit, or particular soullessness. The state of being bourgeois has always existed in the world, and its immortal image is for ever fixed in the gospels with its equally immortal antithesis, but in the nineteenth century it attained its climax and ruled supreme. Though the middle-class society of the last century is so spoken of in the superficial social-economic significance of the term, it is bourgeois in a deeper and more spiritual sense. This middle-class mentality ripened and enslaved human society and culture at the summit of their civilization. Its concupiscence is no longer restricted by man's supernatural beliefs as it was in past epochs, it is no longer kept in bounds by the sacred symbolism of a nobler traditional culture; the bourgeois spirit emancipated itself, expanded, and was at last able to express its own type of life. But even when the triumph of mediocrity was complete a few deep thinkers denounced it with uncompromising power: Carlyle, Nietzsche, Ibsen, Léon Bloy, Dostoievsky, Leontiev—all foresaw the victory of the bourgeois spirit over a truly great culture, on the ruins of which it would establish its own hideous kingdom. With prophetic force and fire these men denounced the spiritual sources and foundations of middle-classdom and, repelled by its ugliness, thirsting for a nobler culture, a different life, looked back upon Greece or the middle ages, the Renaissance or Byzantium. Leontiev has stated the problem strikingly:

> Is it not dreadful and humiliating to think that Moses went up upon Sinai, the Greeks built their lovely temples, the Romans waged their Punic wars, Alexander, that handsome genius in a plumed helmet, fought his battles, apostles preached, martyrs suffered, poets sang, artists painted, knights shone at tournaments—only that some French, German, Russian bourgeois garbed in unsightly and absurd clothes should enjoy life 'individually' or 'collectively' on the ruins of all this vanished splendour?

History has failed, there is no such thing as historical progress, and the present is in no wise an improvement upon the past: there was more beauty in the past. A period of high cultural development is succeeded by another wherein culture deteriorates qualitatively. The will to power, to well-being, to wealth, triumphs over the will to holiness, to genius. The highest spiritual achievements belong to the past, spirituality is on the wane, and a time of spiritual decline is a time of bourgeois ascendancy. The knight and the monk, the philosopher and the poet, have been superseded by a new type—the greedy bourgeois conqueror, organizer, and trader. The centre of life is displaced and transferred to its periphery, the organic hierarchical order of life is being destroyed. In the new machine-made industrial-capitalist civilization of Europe and America the spiritual culture of the old West, based on a sacred symbolism and sacred tradition, is being irrevocably annihilated.

One of those whose rebellion against the bourgeois spirit was most uncompromising and bitter was Léon Bloy, the remarkable and little known French Catholic writer.* Bloy, who lived all his life unrecognized and in dire misery, has written an extraordinary book, *L'Exégèse des Lieux Communs*, which is a searching examination of the commonplaces of

* I wrote an article upon him, "The Knight of Poverty," in the magazine *Sophia*, June 1914.

bourgeois wisdom. He gives a wonderfully witty metaphysical interpretation of the pronouncements which are the bourgeois's rule of life. Thus in "Dieu ne demande pas tant" he endeavours to penetrate the secret movements of the heart, mind, and will of a bourgeois, to expose his peculiar metaphysics and mysticism. The bourgeois, even when he is a "good Catholic," believes only in this world, in the expedient and the useful; he is incapable of living by faith in another world and refuses to base his life on the mystery of Golgotha. "The magnificent superiority of the bourgeois is grounded on unbelief, even *after* he has seen and touched. No! upon the utter impossibility of seeing and touching, due to unbelief." The bourgeois is an idolater, enslaved by the visible. "Idolatry is the preference of the visible to the invisible." "Business" is the bourgeois's god, his absolute. It was the bourgeois who crucified Christ: on Golgotha he cut the world off from Christ, "money" from the poor. The *Poor* and *Money* are great symbols for Bloy. There is a mystery of money, its mysterious separation from the spirit, and the middle-class world is governed by this money bereft of the spirit. Middle-classdom is opposed to the Absolute, it is destructive of eternity. A bourgeois may be religious, and this middle-class religiosity is more hateful in Bloy's eyes than atheism. How many such bourgeois idolaters did he discover amongst "good Catholics"—the Lord Christ is very decorative in shops! Léon Bloy studies the average bourgeois, but the problem can be deepened, for the bourgeois may manifest himself on a superior and more brilliant plane, even in the higher degrees of a spiritual life, where he paralyses all spiritual movement and extinguishes the fire which is the very essence of the spirit.

The bourgeois may be pious, he may even be just, but it was said, "Unless your justice abound more than that of the Scribes and Pharisees, you shall not enter into the kingdom of Heaven." The bourgeois's justice never exceeds that of the Scribes and Pharisees, he loves to give alms "in synagogues and in the streets" so as to be "honoured by men," to "stand and pray in the synagogues and corners of the streets," to be "seen by men"; he loves to judge, and is the first to cast a stone at the sinner. When the disciples plucked ears of wheat on a Sabbath it was the bourgeois who taunted Jesus: "Behold, why do they on the Sabbath-day that which is not lawful?" And the answer he was given was one to upset all middle-class notions: " . . . I tell you that there is here a greater than the temple. And if you knew what this meaneth, *I will have mercy and not sacrifice*, you would never have condemned the innocent. For the Son of Man is lord even of the Sabbath. . . . The Sabbath was made for man, not man for the Sabbath." It was again the bourgeois who said, "The Son of Man is come eating and drinking . . . behold a man that is a glutton and a drinker of wine, a friend of publicans and sinners"; for he has no love for publicans and sinners, his predilections lie with the righteous Pharisees. The bourgeois is convinced that man is defiled by what enters his lips, though it has been said to him, "The things which come out from a man, they defile a man." And, addressing the bourgeois, Christ said, "Amen, I say to you that the publicans and the harlots shall go into the kingdom of God before you. . . . Whosoever shall exalt himself shall be humbled, and he that shall humble himself shall be exalted." But, "Woe to you, Scribes and Pharisees, hypocrites, because you shut the kingdom of Heaven against men; for you yourselves do not enter in and those that are going in you suffer not to enter." And, "Whether is greater, the gold or the temple that sanctifieth the gold?" When the bourgeois remarked that "He eats and drinks with publicans and sinners," Jesus replied, "They that are in health need not a physician, but they that are ill. . . . I am not come to call the just but the sinners." These words of Christ, too, are aimed directly at the bourgeois: "He that will save his life shall lose it: and he that shall lose his life for my sake shall find it. For what doth it profit a man if he gain the whole world and suffer the loss of his own soul?" The bourgeois is out for the conquest of the whole world, and Jesus says to him, "Woe to you . . . because you love the uppermost seats in the synagogues and salutations in the market-place." And his interests in this world are repudiated by Jesus in the words: "Seek not what you shall eat, or what you shal drink . . . for all these things do the nations of the world seek. But your Father knoweth that you have need of these things. But seek ye first the kingdom of God and his justice, and all these things shall be added unto you." A bourgeois heart is condemned: "You . . . outwardly appear to men just, but inwardly are full of hypocrisy and iniquity." Christ said to those whom he chose, "If you had been of the world, the world would love its own; but because you are not of the world but I have chosen you out of the world, therefore the world hateth you." "The world" is the bourgeois spirit: it is not God's creation, the cosmos which the Son of God could not deny, but the enslavement and the overburdening of God's creation by passions and concupiscence. A bourgeois is a man who loves "the world." The eternal repudiation of the very foundations of his spirit is expressed in the words, "Love not the world nor the things which are in the world." To be bourgeois is a bondage, a tie with "the world," an enslavement by it; it involves the rejection of the freedom of the spirit which follows upon liberation from the power of "the world"; it does not accept the mystery of Golgotha, it denies the Cross. Bourgeois consciousness of life is in opposition to the tragic consciousness of life: the man who lives through a tragedy is free from the taint, and in the truly dramatic moments of life a bourgeois ceases to be one.

Wherein are to be found the spiritual roots of this malady? In too strong a faith in this visible world and unbelief in another, invisible world. The bourgeois is impressed with this world of material things, stirred, tempted by it; he does not believe seriously in another existence, in a spiritual being, he feels no confidence in his neighbour's faith. He always thinks, "I know you, you are all just the same as myself, only you refuse to admit it; you pretend and deceive yourselves." All live by the goods of this world, all are crushed by the outward actuality, and so, because he is conscious of this fact and acknowledges it, the bourgeois deems himself superior to his neighbours. He is no symbolist: the viewpoint according to which the entire visible and transitory world is but the symbol of another invisible reality is quite alien to him. He is a naïve realist, and only such a childishly realistic outlook is taken by him seriously. When he is a believer, belonging to some religious denomination, he is again the same artless realist. He may even be orthodox, but he does not connect this "faith" of his with his outlook upon life and the world, which is marked by subservience to "the world," an over-simply realistic acceptance of it. If he is nominally a Catholic, Orthodox, Protestant, the bourgeois would deny Christ, did Christ appear to him, as the Scribes and Pharisees rejected him. The bourgeois has never acknowledged any saint during his lifetime, but only long after canonization and universal acceptance. Middle-classdom is enslavement of the spirit, its crushing by the external hard world, dependence upon the temporary and corruptible, incapacity for breaking through to eternity. The bourgeois is oppressed by the tangible, by what enters into him from outside; he cannot exist without some outward sanction, and authority has primarily been created on his behalf. Whenever he overthrows one authority he immediately sets up another, and submits to it. He is bereft of any spiritual fire, of any spiritual creativeness, but has his own "faith" and superstitions. He cannot believe, because faith is an act of freedom, a creative act of the spirit; denying the eternal, he trusts in the temporal; having no faith in the power of God, he believes in the power of things of this world with a reverence verging on idolatry.

The bourgeois does not always appear to us under the guise of a materialist enthralled by the earthly joys of life: this type is elementary and the least interesting of all. There is a superior type which strives to be the guardian of the spiritual foundations of life, aspires to be the benefactor of mankind, to ensure its happiness, to organize the world for it. There exist conservative bourgeois as well as their revolutionary counterpart. Often the bourgeois is a devotee, with the name of God ever on his lips. It is possible to profess materialism openly, and yet not be a bourgeois in the depth of the heart. When he is a "believer" the bourgeois really believes only in the power of this world of visible things and awaits the good of life only from them; such a one in our days confirms the truth of that saying of middle-class wisdom (analysed by Léon Bloy), "God works no more miracles." He readily admits that God *did* work miracles, but this is only a way of saying that miracles are as impossible as they are absurd. He dislikes miracles, nay, fears them: they might upset all his prospects of an organized life. He lives upon the ready-made and he acquires nothing through a creative spiritual power. His faith calls forth no higher spiritual energy but is expedient for promoting worldly success: the very spirit of eternity is converted into a means for the conquest of the goods of life. From its beginning the sacerdotal caste had a leaning towards the bourgeois: often the leaders' own spirit burnt low, and they dreaded every spiritual movement: thus they betrayed their eternal vocation and paved the way to rebellion against the hierarchical principle itself.

When the bourgeois has stuck to his place too long, impeding the movement of everyone and everything till his power threatens life with inertia, there appears another type, with a greed for power and for the best in life, who says, "Clear out! I want your place." This *parvenu* bourgeois is no improvement upon his predecessor; he is even worse, but during the heyday of his conquest he seems a dare-devil and quite unlike the pompous and steadfast bourgeois of old. The new bourgeois has a still greater greed for power and might, is still more ruthless towards the weak, is more intoxicated by his greatness, importance, and sudden predominance. The feeling of sin which weakened and limited the old type disappears completely with the new. In these last years the Russian communist has expressed this type of bourgeois conqueror, a type sinister in its godlessness. In him the middle-class spirit has shown itself in a purer, stronger, unlimited form; its adepts definitely profess the religion of earthly might, earthly power, earthly happiness. The bourgeois always hungers after the first places, loves "position," and when he secures it his self-satisfaction is boundless. This self-satisfaction is one of his characteristic traits. A weakening of the consciousness of the tragedy of life invariably accompanies his worldly successes. Delighted with himself and his "position," he is unable to attain to the wisdom of Ecclesiastes, "I have seen all the works that are done under the sun; and behold, all is vanity and vexation of spirit." He idolizes vanity and thinks his own works divine: "business" obliterates the object and meaning of life; "business" prevents the bourgeois from seeing the person, nature, the starlit skies. Instead, he is entirely taken up with his "business," his own magnificence. All his will-power is turned exclusively to the organization of existence and he loses the capacity of rejoicing in life. He is an organizer and business-man, and organization kills organic life in him. The new bourgeois expels the old—it is the perennial comedy of history. The new man who has entered on to the scene begins by pretending that he repudiates all middle-classness, that his kingdom will not be a middle-class one: he is a socialist and revolutionary. But soon, very soon, the everlasting bourgeois features, the same in all times and with all peoples, reappear.

The bourgeois spirit is an eternal principle, one of the world-principles which manifest themselves ever under new forms. It does not decrease but increases, and on the summits of European and universal civilization it is at its mightiest. The rich man, spiritually enslaved by his wealth and enslaving others, is a prisoner of "the world," and it is more difficult for him to enter the Kingdom than for a camel to pass through the eye of a needle. But the poor man, envying the rich and spiritually enslaved by the desire of usurping his place and his wealth, is the same bourgeois and his entry into the Kingdom is in no wise easier. Herein is enacted the eternal tragicomedy of history. The middle-class spirit takes possession of every social group, either in the shape of satisfaction with one's own "position" and desire to safeguard it at any cost or in the shape of envy of one's neighbour, desire of a good position and will to attain it *at any cost.* And the historical scene presents the tragi-comical picture of two bourgeois seizing each other by the throat, each imagining that he is defending some particular world opposed to the world of his enemy. In reality it is the same world, the same undying principle. Middle-classness is not determined by man's economic situation but by his spiritual attitude towards this position. Therefore in each class it may be spiritually conquered. The historical process of the creation of a nation, its legislation, economics, customs, idolatry of science, is ruled by middle-class standards, and this explains the fact that in the movement of history there is a certain hopelessness, that all these achievements are unsuccessful.

The bourgeois may exist in every sphere of spiritual life. One can be a bourgeois in religion, science, morals, art. We have spoken of the religious bourgeois whose image is depicted in the sacred books. *In every sphere he wants to* appear *and is powerless to* be. He lives by the seeming and evanescent force of that inert spiritual environment in which he occupies, or wishes to occupy, a "position," and not by the living ontological power of his own personality. When he appears as a scientist or academician he is self-satisfied, pompous, and limited; he adapts science to his own level, dreading the free play of thought and the liberty of the questioning spirit, ignoring intuition. The bourgeois moralist judges severely; his virtue weighs heavily upon everyone, he hates the sinners and publicans, and is the guardian of his neighbours' morals. But the average bourgeois is always somewhat of a moralist. This middle-class moralism may manifest itself under various shapes, from the most conservative to the most destructive and revolutionary; it may suddenly demand the crystallization of life and the cessation of all free movement, or the destruction of the entire world with its whole historical heritage. The bourgeois may be an extreme conservative or an extreme revolutionary, but in both cases he is chained to the visible world and knows no spiritual freedom. There is no grace in moralism, it proceeds from an outward source and is deaf to the music of Heaven. While he makes hell on earth, the bourgeois pretends to be preparing a future earthly paradise. The very idea of rationalization of life, of an absolute social harmony, is a middle-class idea which has to be opposed by the "man from the underworld," the "gentleman with a mocking reactionary face." The tower of Babel was built by the bourgeois; the spirit of Socialism is middle-class. An excessive desire of life causes enslavement to the goods of the earth; the overcoming of middle-classdom means a victory over the intensified will directed to "the world." Everything the bourgeois touches, the family, the state, morality, religion, science, all is deadened. Contemplation, which could set him free, is unknown to him. The paradox of his life consists in his repudiation of tragedy; he is weighed down and darkened by his non-acceptance of the internal tragedy of life, of Golgotha; there is a relief and freedom in the acceptance of the Cross and the pain and suffering this entails. Because the bourgeois's consciousness of guilt and sin has become so weak he is the slave of "the world," and his ideal is that of worldly power and wealth: the mystery of Golgotha is unacceptable to him. The bourgeois spirit is nothing but the rejection of Christ; even those whose lips confess him may be the first to crucify him anew.

When the tragic consciousness of guilt, of the tension between the temporal and the eternal, is defeated by the concupiscence of life, power, and enjoyment, this spirit reigns supreme. This concupiscence was the moving principle of the civilization of the nineteenth and early twentieth centuries and, however radically it may have reformed itself, this civilization remains as it was, a middle-class civilization. The ancient symbolical cultures, founded upon sacred myths, had never been so bourgeois in spirit as the pragmatic civilization of modern times, whose might is growing and spreading. Formerly the bourgeois was a psychological type, now he is the socially predominant type. But even in ancient times a middle-class civilization, striving to displace a sacred culture, was fighting its way to the surface. The Prophets branded its spirit with words of fire: "Their land also is filled with silver and gold, and there is no end of their treasures and their land is filled with horses, neither is there any end of their chariots"; but "the lofty looks of man shall be humbled and the haughtiness of men shall be bowed down, and the Lord alone shall be exalted in that day. For the day of the Lord of Hosts shall be upon every one that is proud and lofty, and upon every one that is lifted up; and he shall be brought low. . . . And the loftiness of man shall be bowed down and the haughtiness of men shall be made low and the Lord alone shall be exalted in that day." Jeremiah speaks of a bourgeois civilization: "Run ye to and fro through the streets of Jerusalem, and see now and know and seek in the broad places thereof if ye can find a man, if there be any that executeth judgement, that seeketh the truth, and I will pardon it." The worship of Baal marked the beginning and was a figure of all bourgeois civilizations, which invariably destroy a sacred culture: "Thus saith the Lord: Cursed be the man that trusteth in man and maketh flesh his arm and whose heart departeth from the Lord"; and its victory is thus spoken of: "Babylon hath been a golden cup in the Lord's hand that made all the earth drunken; the nations have drunken of her wine, therefore the nations are mad." It was there in Babylon that appeared the first middle-class civilization recorded by history, and it dominated the whole East. Its spirit was vigorously denounced by Ezekiel: "Her princes in the midst thereof are like wolves ravening the prey, to shed blood and to destroy souls, to get dishonest gain . . . the people of the land have used oppression and exercised robbery, and have vexed the poor and needy: yea, they have oppressed the stranger wrongfully." And, "Woe be to the shepherds of Israel that do feed themselves! . . . The diseased have ye not strengthened, neither have ye healed that which was sick, neither have ye bound up that which was broken, neither have ye brought again that which was driven away, neither have ye sought that which was lost; but with force and with cruelty have ye ruled them." To the vision of the ancient prophets were revealed the catastrophes which would inevitably follow upon the triumph of the bourgeois spirit. Such a civilization is conceived within the womb of a developing culture, the bourgeois type begins to predominate, and its spirit contaminates rulers, guides, and priests. It is then that the nations and their cultures are threatened by disaster—the wrath of God falls upon them.

But antiquity knew only a tendency towards the bourgeois spirit, it never saw its final triumph. It was left to our European culture to accomplish its victory and give the world's destinies into the hands of the bourgeois. The increase of populations and their unlimited needs, the will to life, to power, to domination, have brought about this triumph: but our civilization cannot endure; the bourgeois is destructive of eternity, and therefore he is not its inheritor. Men have long anticipated the doom of European civilization. In the impending cataclysms the new revolutionary bourgeois will attempt to spread his domination the world over, to make his spirit universal, to exalt it as the pearl of creation. But eternity does not belong to it. The hour will come when the Lord will say, "Behold, I, even I, will both search my sheep and seek them out!"

Spirit alone can defeat the bourgeois condition; no material means will avail. It is not a material or economic phenomenon, industrial development as such is not bourgeois. This does not mean that the material structure of society is indifferent and cannot assume a bourgeois character, but that the bourgeois structure of a society is merely the expression of a bourgeois spirit, of a false direction of the will. It is a wrong conception of life, the concupiscence of the temporal, which transforms life into an inferno. In its finite and vivid type the bourgeois is an apocalyptic image, a figure of the coming kingdom of which the sacred scripture has spoken. The middle-class spirit is contrasted with the pilgrim spirit: in this world Christians are but wayfarers, and the inner feeling of this pilgrimage is inherent to the Christian in every walk of life. A Christian has no city—he is in quest of the City of God, which can never be the city of "this world"; whenever an earthly city is mistaken for the New Jerusalem, Christians cease to be pilgrims and the bourgeois spirit reigns supreme.

II

MAN AND MACHINE

MAN AND MACHINE

I

It is not an exaggeration to say that the question of technique has now become that of the destiny of man and of his culture in general. In this age of spiritual turpitude, when not only the old religious beliefs but also the humanist creed of the nineteenth century have been shaken, civilized man's sole strong belief is in the might of technical science and its capacity for infinite development. Technique is man's last love, for the sake of which he is prepared to change his very image. Contemporary events only strengthen this faith. In order to believe, man craved for miracles, though doubting their possibility: now he witnesses technique actually work "miracles." This problem is an anxious one for Christian consciousness, though Christians have not yet fully realized its meaning: they have two ways of considering it, and both are inadequate. For the overwhelming majority technique, from the viewpoint of religion, is neutral and indifferent; it concerns specialists, adds to the amenities of life, and its boons are equally enjoyed by Christians as by others, but it is a special domain, by no means encroaching upon the reason and conscience of a Christian as such; it raises no spiritual problem. On the other hand, a Christian minority views it in an apocalyptic light, is terrified by its increasing power over human life, sees in it the triumph of the spirit of Antichrist, the beast "coming up out of the earth." Such an abuse of the Apocalypse is especially proper to the Russian Orthodox: anything they dislike, anything which destroys the customary, is freely interpreted by them as a victory of Antichrist and the imminent fulness of time. This is a lazy solution, arising from fear, though the first solution, that of neutrality, is quite as indolent—it simply refuses to perceive any problem at all.

Technique may be understood in a broader and narrower way. *τέχνη* stands both for industry and art, *τεχνάζω* means to make, to create with skill. We speak not only of an economic, industrial, military technique, a technique of transport and the comforts of life, but also of a technique of thought, versification, painting, dancing, law, even of a spiritual technique, a mystical way: thus, for example, Yoga is a peculiar spiritual technique. Technique seeks to attain in everything the greatest results with the minimum expenditure of power; such is especially the technique of our mechanical, economic age. But in it quantitative attainments replace the qualitative that characterized the master-artisan of ancient cultures. In his last slender book,

Der Mensch und die Technik, Spengler defines technique not as a tool but as a struggle—undoubtedly technique is always a means, a weapon, and not an end. There can be no technical ends of life, only technical means: the ends of life belong to another sphere, to that of the spirit. Very often the aims of life are superseded by its means, which then usurp so important a place in human life as completely to eliminate its ultimate object from man's consciousness. This is what is happening on a vast scale to-day. Naturally for a scientist, given to scientific discoveries, or an engineer, concerned with inventions, technique may become the principal object and end of life; in such cases, being knowledge and invention, technique becomes endowed with a spiritual meaning and pertains to the life of the spirit. But the substitution of the aims of life by technical means must be equivalent to the diminution and extinction of the spirit, and this is what we are witnessing. A technical weapon is by nature heterogeneous, not only to the one who uses it but also to that for which it is being used; it is heterogeneous to man, to his spirit and reason. Therein lies the fatal enslavement of human life by technique. The very definition of man as *homo faber*, a tool-using being, so common in the history of civilization, already shows the supersession of the ends of life by its means. Man is certainly an engineer, but he invented the art of engineering for aims transcending its limits, and here we witness a repetition of Marx's materialistic conception of history. Economics are a necessary condition of life, no intellectual and spiritual life, no ideology, are thinkable without an economic basis, yet the object and meaning of human life are in nowise contained in this necessary basis. What appears to be strongest because of its urgency and necessity is not the most valuable and, contrarywise, what stands supreme in the hierarchy of values is not at all the most powerful. We might say that in our world the strongest appears to be coarse matter, though it is also the least valuable, and in our sinful world the least powerful seems to be God. He was crucified by the world, yet he is the Supreme Value.* Technique is so powerful nowadays precisely because it does not represent a supreme value.

We are confronted by a fundamental paradox: without technique culture is impossible, its very growth is dependent upon it, yet a final victory of technique, the advent of a technical age, brings the destruction of culture. The technical and the natural-organic elements are ever present in culture, and the definite victory of the former over the latter signifies the transformation of culture into something which no longer bears any likeness to it. A technical epoch demands from man the making of things in

* N. Hartman in his *Ethik* writes finely on the theme that supreme values are often the less powerful.

great quantities with the least expenditure of power, and man becomes an instrument of production: the thing is placed above man. Romanticism is a reaction of the natural-organic element of culture against its technical element; in so far as romanticism rebels against the classical consciousness it rebels against the preponderance of the technical form over Nature. A return to Nature is a perennial feature in the history of culture; it expresses the fear of its own destruction by technique, the end of the integrity of human nature; romanticism also strives after integrity and organic order. The longing for a return to Nature is but a reminiscence of the lost Paradise, a craving to go back to it, but man's return to Paradise is always obstructed.

The history of our race can be divided into three epochs, the natural-organic, the cultural in the proper sense, and the technical-mechanical. To these epochs correspond the different relations of spirit to Nature, namely the diffusion of spirit in Nature, the emergence of spirit from Nature and formation of a special spiritual sphere; lastly, spirit's active conquest of Nature and domination over it. Of course these stages are not to be taken exclusively in a chronological sequence: they are primarily different types. In the cultural epoch man still lived in the natural world, not made by him but which appeared to have been created by God. He was tied to the earth, the plants, and the animals, and tellurgical mysticism—the mysticism of earth—played an enormous part. We know the great significance of the vegetative and animalistic religions, the transfigured elements of which can be detected in Christianity: Christians believe that man was created from earth, and to earth shall he return. Culture at the height of its development was still encompassed by Nature; it loved gardens and beasts, flowers, shady parks and meadows, rivers and lakes, pedigree dogs and horses, birds—all these belonged to culture. Men of that time, however distant they may have been from a natural life, still gazed at the sky, the stars, the fleeting clouds . . . contemplation of the beauties of Nature is predominantly a sign of culture. Culture, the State, modes of life, all were understood organically by analogy with the life of organic beings; the flourishing of cultures and States appeared to be somewhat in the nature of a vegetative-animal process. Culture was full of symbols: in shapes of earth it reflected heaven, prefigured another world. Technique knows no symbols; it is realistic, reflects nothing, creates only new actualities; it is plainly visible in its entirety, and divorces man from Nature and from other worlds.

Our fundamental thesis consists in the distinction between organism and organization. The former, generated by natural cosmic life, continues the process of generation; this generation is the characteristic sign of an organism. Organization, on the other hand, is neither generated nor capable of generating: it is a creation of man's activity, is made, though this making is not the supreme form of creation. Organism is not an aggregate of parts, it is integral and born entire; in it the whole precedes the parts and is present in every part,* it grows and develops. Mechanism, evolved by an organizing process, is composed of parts, it can neither grow nor develop; no integrity exists in its parts, nor does it precede them. An organism possesses a *raison d'être*, immanently pertaining to it and given it by the Creator or by Nature, and is determined by the preponderance of the whole over its parts. But the *raison d'être* of an organization is of a very different kind, and has been given it from outside by the organizer. A mechanism is constructed in view of a definite end but has no final cause proper to it. A watch works very appositely, nevertheless the intention for which it works is not in the watch itself but in the man who made and wound it up. An organized mechanism depends on its organizer for its purpose, yet it possesses an inertia which may react upon the organizer and even enslave him. History records organized bodies bearing a similitude with living organisms. Thus the patriarchal order with its natural economics appeared to be organic and even everlasting, an order created by Nature

* See Driesch's *La Philosophie de l'organisme.*

itself or by its Creator, but not by man. For a long time men believed in the existence of an eternal objective order of Nature with which human life had to be brought into harmony and subordination. The natural was taken as a norm—all that was in accordance with it was good and just. A fixed cosmos, an hierarchical system, an eternal *ordo* existed for ancient Greek and medieval man, for Aristotle and for St. Thomas Aquinas; earth and Heaven constituted an immutable hierarchical system, and the very idea of a permanent order of Nature was connected with an objective teleological principle. And now technique, in the shape it has assumed since the end of the eighteenth century, destroys this faith in an everlasting order of Nature and destroys it in a far more thorough way than is achieved even by evolutionism. Evolutionism mainly originated from biological sciences, and therefore development was understood as an organic process; it admitted changes, though such were effected within the natural order. We are now living in an age of physical and not biological sciences, the age of Einstein and not of Darwin, and physical sciences are not so favourable to an organic conception of the life of Nature as were biological sciences. Though in the second half of the nineteenth century biology itself was mechanistic, still it inclined towards an organic conception in other spheres, such as sociology. Naturalism, as it shaped itself at that time, admitted a development in Nature within its own eternal order, and therefore it laid greater stress upon the principle of the regularity of natural processes, a principle contemporary science is much less concerned with. The natural reality with which technique confronts man is in no wise a result of evolution but is the outcome of man's own inventiveness and creative activity, not of an organic but of an organizing process: herein lies the significance of the entire technical epoch. *The supremacy of technique and the machine is primarily a transition from organic to organized life, from growth to construction.* From the viewpoint of organic life technique spells disincarnation, a cleavage between the flesh and the spirit in the organic bodies of history. Technique inaugurates a new stage of actuality and this actuality is man's work, the result of the incursion of spirit into Nature and the introduction of reason into elemental processes. Technique destroys ancient bodies and the new ones it creates do not resemble organic bodies; they are organized bodies.

The tragedy consists in the rebellion of creation against its Creator. It is the mystery of the fall of man, which repeats itself throughout the history of mankind. Man's promethean spirit is unable to master the technique created to curb unloosed and unforeseen energies. We see this in every process of "rationalization" whereby man is replaced by machine. In social life technique substitutes the organic and irrational by the organized and rational, which results in new irrational consequences; e.g. industrial rationalization breeds unemployment, the greatest evil of the day. The substitution of man's work by the machine is a positive gain which ought to lead to the abolition of human slavery and poverty, but machinery refuses to comply with man's demands and dictates its own laws. Says man to machine, "I need you in order to ease my life and increase my power," and the machine retorts, "I don't need you at all. I shall make everything without you; you may perish so far as I am concerned." Taylor's system is the extreme form of rationalization of labour, and it also transforms man into an improved machine. The machine demands that man assume its image; but man, created to the image and likeness of God, cannot become such an image, for to do so would be equivalent to his extermination. Here we are confronted with the limits of the transition from the organic and irrational to the organized and rational. An organization, bound up with technique, presupposes an organizing subject, namely, an organism which cannot be transformed into a machine (though any organization tends to mechanize its organizer). The very spirit which created technique and machinery cannot be completely technicalized and mechanized, some irrational principle will ever survive. The titanic struggle of man against the Nature he has mechanized is contained in this endeavour to rationalize spirit and transform it into an automaton. In the beginning man depended upon Nature and this dependence was vegetative and animal; then began a new dependence. This provides the acuteness of the whole problem, for man's organism, his psycho-physical nature, has evolved in another world and adapted itself to the old Nature and he has not yet adapted himself to the new actuality which manifests itself through technique and machinery. He cannot even foresee whether he will be able to live in this new electrical and radio-active atmosphere, in these frigid metallic surroundings devoid of all animal warmth; we do not know whether this environment may not prove deadly to him, as some physicians declare it will. Moreover, human inventiveness in the matter of destructive engines very much exceeds its discoveries in medicine; it is easier to invent a poison-gas by which millions of lives may be wiped out than to find a cure for cancer or tuberculosis. Man is powerless before his own inventions—discoveries within the sphere of organic life are far more difficult than those in the inorganic world, which is a world of wonders.

II

The reign of technique and machinery was unforeseen in the classification of sciences, and it is an actuality very dissimilar to the mechanical and physico-chemical realities. This new actuality is seen only in the historical perspective of civilization, and not through Nature. In the cosmic process it develops later than all other stages of civilization, coming at its highest point and after a complete social development. Art was also instrumental in creating actualities inexistent in Nature: heroes and images depicted by art represent a particular kind of reality—Don Quixote, Hamlet, Faust, Leonardo's Mona Lisa, a symphony by Beethoven, are new realities, not pertaining to Nature. They have an existence, a fate of their own, and their influence upon men has very complex consequences. Cultured people dwell amidst these realities and, in so far as it is manifested in art, reality bears a symbolic character, it reflects a world of ideas. Technique, on the other hand, builds up a reality lacking any symbolism whatever and reality is imparted by it directly. This fact reacts upon art, for technique transforms art itself, as is manifested by the cinema gradually superseding the theatre. The cinematograph's tremendous influence cannot be overrated and is wholly due to technical inventions, chiefly to discoveries in the fields of light and sound which would have seemed miraculous to men of a former age; it dominates space and conquers oceans, deserts, hills, as it conquers time itself. Through it and the wireless the actor and the singer address not a restricted audience but vast masses of people in all parts of the globe, in all countries, and of every race. It constitutes a most powerful weapon for uniting mankind—and it may be used for the basest and most vulgar ends. It witnesses to the power of realization inherent in contemporary technique; a new actuality is inaugurated and this actuality, connected with technique radically revolutionizing relations to space and time, is a creation of man's spirit, of his reason, of his will. It is a super-physical reality, neither spiritual nor psychic but precisely super-physical, for there is such a sphere as there is also a super-psychical one.

Technique possesses a universal significance, for through it a new cosmos comes into being. In his recent book, *Réflexions sur la science des machines,* Lafitte says that beside inorganic and organic bodies there exists also another realm, that of organized bodies—the world of machinery. It is a new category of being, for the machine is neither inorganic nor organic and its appearance is connected with a difference between the two qualities. It is erroneous to class the machine with the inorganic on the strength of the elements of inorganic bodies that enter into its composition.

Inorganic Nature knows no machinery. Organized bodies belong to a social world; they did not precede man (as did inorganic bodies) but came after and through him. Man was able to bring into being a new actuality, thereby manifesting a terrifying power which bears witness to his creative and royal vocation in the world—as it also manifests his weakness and inclination to slavery. The machine has a tremendous significance, not sociological only but also cosmological, and it raises with particular acuteness the problem of the destiny of man in society and in the universe, a problem of his relation to Nature, of the individual's to society, of the spirit's to matter, of the irrational to the rational. It is indeed amazing that up to now there has been no philosophy of technique and of machinery; though many books have been written on the subject and much preliminary work for such a philosophy has been done, the essential has yet to be accomplished. The machine and technique have not been studied as a spiritual problem bearing upon the fate of man, but only examined from without, in its social projection. From within it is the theme of the philosophy of man's very existence (*Existenzphilosophie*). Can man live only in the old physical and organic cosmos which seemed to have a fixed order, or can he survive in a new one, as yet unknown? Christianity, with which human destiny is bound up, is faced by a new world but has not yet appreciated the position. Upon this depends the very existence of a philosophy of technique for the question must first be solved by philosophical knowledge: it has always been so, though philosophy has failed to realize it.*

What, then, is the meaning of this technical age and the beginning of a new universe for the destiny of man? Does it spell materialization and the destruction of spirit and all spirituality, or may it have some other significance? The break of the spirit from the old organic life, the mechanization of existence, convey an impression that spirituality is dying in the world—never has materialism been so strong. The close connection of spirit with historical bodies, which technique is destroying, appeared to be of an everlasting order and many believe, too, that spirit disappears after its separation from flesh. The technical age rings the knell of a good many things. The Soviet technical building, for example, produces a particularly sinister impression; its originality is not in the technique as such—there is nothing very surprising about that: America has gone much further and it would be difficult to catch up with her. No; the original aspect of communist Russia is the kind of *spirituality* underlying its technical construction. This indeed is something unusual, the manifestation of a new spiritual type which produces

* Friedrich Dessauer's *Philosophie der Technik* represents an attempt to give a philosophy of technique.

so ominous an impression by its eschatology, which is the very reverse of Christian. In themselves technique and economics may be neutral, but the relation of spirit to them inevitably becomes a spiritual problem. At times it would seem that we are living in an age when technique predominates over wisdom, in the ancient noble sense of that word. Christian eschatology connects the transfiguration of the world with the action of the divine Spirit; technical eschatology awaits a final possession of and domination over it by means of machinery. Therefore, though the answer to the question of the significance of the technical age from the Christian and spiritual viewpoint seems to be clear and simple, in reality it is very complex. Technique is as dual in its significance as everything else in this world; it separates man from the earth and deals a deadly blow to all mysticism of the earth, to the mysticism of the maternal principle which has played so important a part in human society. The actualism and titanism of technique is in direct opposition to a passive, vegetative, animal existence in the womb of the *Magna Mater*, it destroys the cosiness and warmth of organic life clinging to the soil. *The meaning of the technical age is primarily that it closes the tellurgical period of human history, when man was determined by the earth not only in the physical but also in the metaphysical sense.* Herein lies the religious meaning of technique. It gives man a planetary feeling of the earth, very different from the one he experienced in former ages. He feels differently when his feet touch the depth, holiness, mysticism of the earth than when he sees it as a planet flying into infinite space amidst innumerable universes, and he himself able to detach himself from it, to fly into the air, into the stratosphere. Theoretically this change of consciousness took place at the beginning of modern history when the system of Copernicus superseded Ptolemy's and, the infinity of worlds being discovered, the earth was no longer considered as the physical centre of the universe. Pascal was terrified by this as yet only theoretical speculation, the silence of space and of endless worlds overawed him. The cosmos of antiquity and of the middle ages, of Thomas Aquinas and Dante, vanished, and man found a compensation and fulcrum by transferring the centre of gravity to himself, his own *ego*—the subject. The idealistic modern philosophy is an expression of this compensation for the loss of a cosmos within which man had his own hierarchical place and felt himself surrounded by higher forces. But technique possesses a mighty power of realization and imparts an acute awareness of the destruction of that universe of which our earth was the centre. This revolutionizes the entire life of contemporary man, and in relation to him its result is contradictory and dual. When the infinity of space and universes was first revealed he was terrified: he felt lost and humbled—he was no longer the central point of all but an insignificant, infinitely small grain of dust. The might of technique proceeds with this revelation of the limitless space into which our planet is hurled, but at the same time imparts to man an impression of his own power and of the possibility of conquering this limitless universe. At last, and for the first time, man is king and master of the earth and, maybe, of the universe. His relation to space and time undergoes a radical change. Formerly he clung to mother earth lest he be crushed by them; now he no more dreads separation from the earth, but on the contrary he wants to fly off as far as possible into space. This manifests man's maturity; he is no longer in need of a mother's care and protection. On the one hand technique adds to the comforts and luxuries of life; on the other it makes the struggle more grim—these two aspects are inseparable.

Past cultures only attained restricted areas and limited human groups, whether that of classical Greece or of Italy during the Renaissance, France in the seventeenth or Germany in the early nineteenth century. This shows the aristocratic, qualitative principle of culture; it was unable to deal with large quantities, it lacked adequate methods; whereas technique conquers boundless spaces and holds masses of people under its sway: everything is on a universal scale and intended to reach mankind as a whole. In this lies its cosmological significance. Its very principle is democratic: a technical era is an age of democracy and socialization in which everything is collectivized. In the ancient cultures men led a vegetative organic life, and such a life, sanctioned by religion, did not require the organization of people at large as we understand it nowadays; an order, even a very stable one, could exist without organization in its modern meaning—it existed organically. Technique makes man conscious of his own awful power and promotes a will to might and expansion. This will, which produced European capitalism, inevitably brings "the masses" on to the stage of history and results in the collapse of the old organic order, which is superseded by the new organization created by technique. Undeniably this new form of mass organization, this technicalization of life, does away with the beauty of the old life. It kills all individuality, all originality; it becomes impersonal, for mass-production is anonymous. Not only the external plastic aspect of life but also the internal emotional side lose their individuality. We can understand the romantic reaction from technique, the revolt of Ruskin and Tolstoy, the motives of which were both æsthetic and moral—yet this repudiation of it is hopeless and cannot be consistently pursued: it reduces itself to a defence of more primitive and obsolete forms, and not to its wholesale denial. Everyone is now reconciled to the steam-engine and the railways, yet there was a time when they raised a storm of protest. You may denounce and abstain from air-traffic, but you certainly travel by rail and motor-car; you may detest the underground, yet journey by bus or tram; you refuse to be reconciled to the "talkies," whilst enjoying the "movies"! We are inclined to idealize the past which ignored machinery, and this is very natural in our ugly, stuffy times. But we choose to overlook the fact that the old pre-technique life was based on an abominable exploitation of human beings, on slavery and serfdom, and that the machine may be an instrument of liberation from this exploitation and slavery.

In the matter of this idealization of the past we encounter the paradox of time. The past which we so much admire has never really existed—it is but a creation of our own imagination which cleanses it from all evil and ugliness. The past we so love belongs to eternity and never existed in bygone ages: it is merely a composite part of our present; there was another present in the past as it actually was, a present with all its own evils and shadows. This means that we can only love that which is eternal, and therefore we cannot want to go back to the past any more than there can be a return to it. We may only long for a return to what was eternal in the past, but this eternal element has been singled out by us in the transfiguring creative act and been shorn of all its darker aspects. We cannot dream of going back to a natural economy and patriarchal order, to a predominance of husbandry and crafts, as Ruskin dreamed. This possibility is not given to man: he has to fulfil his destiny, and the human masses which have stepped on to the historical stage demand new forms of organization, new equipment. However, what we call the "technical era" is not eternal either: this unheard-of domination of technique over the human soul will end—but not by the denial of all technique: it will end by subordination to spirit. Man can neither remain tied to the soil and entirely dependent upon it nor tear himself free altogether and fly into space; some link with earth will remain, as husbandry will remain—man is unable to exist without it. Till the end of time and the final transfiguration of the world man will not regain his lost paradise, though he will ever retain a longing for it and see its image in art and Nature. This intimate link binding man to the soul of Nature is another aspect of his relations with it; the final casting-out of Nature by technical actuality perverts not Nature only but man himself. It is impossible to visualize the future of mankind integrally; it will be composite, it will know reactions from technique and machinery and returns to primeval Nature—but technique and machinery will never be altogether done away with whilst man pursues his earthly journey.

III

Wherein consists the menace of the machine to man, the danger now so clearly apparent? I doubt if it threatens spirit and the spiritual life, but the machine and technique deal terrible blows to man's emotional side, to human feeling, which is on the wane in contemporary civilization. Whereas the old culture threatened man's body, which it neglected and often debilitated, mechanical civilization endangers the heart, which can scarcely bear the contact of cold metal and is unable to live in metallic surroundings. The process of the destruction of the heart as the centre of emotional life is characteristic of our times. In the works of such outstanding French writers as Proust and Gide the heart as an integral organ of man's emotional life is inexistent, everything has been decomposed into the intellectual element and sensual feelings. Keyserling is right when he speaks of the destruction of the emotional order in modern civilization and longs for its restoration.* Technique strikes fiercely at humanism, the humanist conception of the world, the humanist ideal of man and culture. It seems surprising at first to be told that technique is not so dangerous to spirit, yet we may in truth say that ours is the age of technique and spirit, not an age of

* See his *Méditations Sud-Americaines*.

the heart. The religious significance of contemporary technique consists precisely in the fact that it makes everything a spiritual problem and may lead to the spiritualization of life, for it demands an intensification of spirituality.

Technique has long ceased to be neutral, to be indifferent to spirit and its problems, and after all, can anything really be neutral? Some things may appear so at a casual glance but, whilst technique is fatal to the heart, it produces a powerful reaction of the spirit. Through technique man becomes a universal creator, for his former arms seem like childish toys in comparison with the weapons it places in his hands now. This is especially apparent in the field of military technique. The destructive power of the weapons of old was very limited and localized; with cannon, muskets, and sabres neither great human masses nor large towns could be destroyed nor could the very existence of civilization be threatened. All this is now feasible. Peaceful scientists will be able to promote cataclysms not only on a historical but on a cosmic scale; a small group possessing the secrets of technical inventions will be able to tyrannize over the whole of mankind; this is quite plausible, and was foreseen by Renan. When man is given power whereby he may rule the world and wipe out a considerable part of its inhabitants and their culture, then everything depends upon man's spiritual and moral standards, on the question: In whose name will he use this power—of what spirit is he?

Thus we see that this problem of technique inevitably becomes a spiritual and ultimately a religious one, and the future of the human race is in the balance. The miracles of technique are always double, and demand an intensification of the spirit infinitely greater than in former cultural ages. Man's spirituality can no more be organically vegetative; we are faced by the demands of a new heroism, internal and external. Our heroism, bound up with warfare in old times, is now no more; it scarcely existed in the last war; technique demands a new kind of heroism, and we are constantly hearing and reading of its manifestations—scientists leaving their laboratories and studies and flying into the stratosphere or diving to the bottom of the ocean. Human heroism is now connected with cosmic spheres. But primarily, a strong spirit is needed in order to safeguard man from enslavement and destruction through technique, and in a certain sense we may say it is a question of life or death. We are sometimes haunted by a horrible nightmare: a time may come when machinery will have attained so great a perfection that man would have governed the world through it had he not altogether disappeared from the earth; machines will be working independently, without a hitch and with a maximum of efficiency and results; the last men will become like machines, then they will vanish, partly because they will be unnecessary and also because they will be unable to live and breathe any longer in the mechanized atmosphere; factories will be turning out goods at great speed and aeroplanes will be flying all over the earth; the wireless will be carrying the sound of music and singing and the speech of the men that once lived; nature will be conquered by technique and this new actuality will be a part of cosmic life. But man himself will be no more, organic life will be no more—a terrible Utopia! It rests with man's spirit to escape this fate. The exclusive power of technical organization and machine-production is tending towards its goal—inexistence within technical perfection. But we cannot admit an autonomous technique with full freedom of action: it *has* to be subordinated to spirit and the spiritual values of life—as everything else has to be. Only upon one condition can the human spirit cope with this tremendous problem: it must not be isolated and dependent only upon itself—it must be united to God. Then only can man preserve the image and likeness of his Maker and be himself preserved. There is the divergence between Christian and technical eschatology.

IV

The power of technique in human life results in a very great change in the prevalent type of religiousness, and we must admit that this is all for the good. In a mechanical age the hereditary, customary, formal, socially-established sort of religion is weakened; the religiously-minded man feels less tied to traditional forms, his life demands a spiritually intensified Christianity, free from social influences. Religious life tends to become more personal, it is more painfully attained, and this is not individualism, for the universality and mystical unity of religious consciousness are not sociological.

Yet in another respect the domination of technique may be fatal for religious and spiritual life. Technique conquers time and radically alters our relations to it: man becomes capable of mastering time, but technical actuality subordinates him and his inward life to time's accelerating movement. In the crazy speed of contemporary civilization not one single instant is an end in itself and not a single moment can be fixed as being outside time. There is no exit into an instant (*Augenblick*) in the sense Kirkegaard speaks of it: every moment must speedily be replaced by the next, all remaining in the stream of time and therefore ephemeral. Within each moment there seems to be nothing but motion towards the next one: in itself it is void. Such a conquest of time through speed becomes an enslavement to the current of time, which means that in this relation technical activity is destructive of eternity. Man has no time for it, since what is demanded of him is the quickest passage to the succeeding instant. This does not mean that we must see in the past the eternal which is being destroyed by the future: the past does not belong to eternity any more than does the future—both are in time. In the past, as in the future and at all times, an exit into eternity, the self-sufficient complete instant, is always possible. Time obeys the speed-machine, but is not mastered and conquered by it, and man is faced by the question: Will he remain capable of experiencing moments of pure contemplation, of eternity, truth, beauty, God? Unquestionably man has an active vocation in the world and there is truth in action, but he is also a being capable of contemplation in which there is an element determining his *ego*. The very act of man's contemplation, his relation to God, contains a creative deed. The formulation of this problem more than ever convinces us that all the ills of modern civilization are due to the discrepancy between the organization of man's soul inherited from other ages and the new technical, mechanical actuality from which he cannot escape. The human soul is unable to stand the speed which contemporary civilization demands and which tends to transform man himself into a machine. It is a painful process. Contemporary man endeavours to strengthen his body through sports, thus fighting anthropological regression. We cannot deny the positive value of sport whereby man reverts to the old Hellenic view of the body, yet sport may become a means of destruction; it will create distortion instead of harmony if not subordinated to his integral idea. By its nature technical civilization is impersonal; it demands man's activity, whilst denying him the right to a personality, and therefore he experiences an immense difficulty in surviving in such a civilization. In every way *person* is in opposition to *machine*, for person is primarily unity in multiplicity and integrity, it is its own end and refuses to be transformed into a part, a means, an instrument. On the other hand, technical civilization and mechanized society demand that man should be that and nothing else: they strive to destroy his unity and integrity or, in other words, deny him his personality. A fight to the death between this civilization and society and the human person is inevitable; it will be man *versus* machine. Technique is pitiless to all that lives and exists, and therefore concern for the living and existing has to restrict the power of technique over life.

The machine-mind triumphing in a capitalist civilization begins by perverting the hierarchy of values, and the reinstatement of that hierarchy marks the limitation of the power of the machine. This cannot be done by a reversion to the old structure of the soul and the former natural and organic actuality.* The character of modern technical civilization and its influence upon man is inacceptable not only to Christian consciousness but also to man's natural dignity. We are faced by the task of saving the very image of man. He has been called to continue creation and his work represents the eighth day: he was called to be king and master of the earth, yet the work he is doing and to which he was called enslaves him and defaces his image. So a new man appears, with a new structure of the soul, a new image. The man of former days believed himself to be the everlasting man; he was mistaken, for though he possessed an eternal principle he was not eternal: the past is not eternity. A new man is due to appear in the world and the problem consists in the question, not of his relation to the old man, but of his relation to everlasting man, to the eternal in him—and this eternal principle is the divine image and likeness whereby he becomes a *person*. This is not to be understood statically, for the divine image in man, as in a natural being, is manifested and confirmed dynamically—in this consists the endless struggle against

* The important book of Cina Lombroso, *La rançon du machinisme*, displays too great a faith in the possibility of a return to a pre-mechanical civilization.

the old man in the name of the new man. But the machine-age strives to replace the image and likeness of God by the image and likeness of the machine, and this does not mean the creation of a new man but the destruction and disappearance of man, his substitution by another being with another, non-human, existence. Man created the machine, and this may give him a grand feeling of his own dignity and power, but this pride imperceptibly and gradually leads to his humiliation. All through history man has been changing, he has always been old and new, but throughout the ages he was in contact with eternity and remained *man.* The new man will finally break away from eternity, will definitely fasten on to the new world he has to possess and conquer, and will cease to be human, though at first he will fail to realize the change. We are witnessing man's dehumanization, and the question is: Is he to be or not to be, not the ancient man who has to be outlived, but just simply *man?* From the very dawn of human consciousness as manifested in the Bible and in ancient Greece this problem has never been posited with such depth and acuteness. European humanism believed in the eternal foundations of human nature, and inherited this belief from the Greco-Roman world. Christianity believes man to be God's creation, bearing his image and likeness and redeemed by his divine Son. Both these faiths strengthen European man, who believes himself to be universal, but now they have been shaken; the world is being dehumanized as well as dechristianized by the monstrous power of technique.

This power, like that of the machine, is bound up with capitalism; it originated in the very womb of the capitalist order, and the machine was the strongest weapon for its development. Communism has taken over these things wholesale from capitalist civilization and made a veritable religion of the machine: it worships it as a totem. Undoubtedly, since technique has created capitalism it may also help to conquer it and to create a less unjust social order: it may become a mighty arm in the solution of the social problem. But all will depend on the question, which spirit predominates, of which spirit man will be. Materialistic communism subordinates the problem of man, as a being composed of soul and body, to the problem of society; it is not for man to organize society, but for society to organize man. The truth is the other way about—primacy belongs to man; it is he who has to organize society and the world, and its organization is dependent upon his spirit. Here man is taken not as an individual being but as a social being with a social vocation to fulfil, since only then has he an active and creative vocation. In our days it is usual to hear people, victims of the machine, accuse it, making it responsible for their crippling; this only humiliates man and does not correspond to his dignity. It is not machinery, which is merely man's creation and consequently irresponsible, that is to be blamed, and it is unworthy to transfer responsibility from man to a machine. Man alone is to blame for the awful power that threatens him; it is not the machine which has despiritualized him—he did it himself. The problem has to be transferred from the outward to the inward. A limitation of the power of technique and machinery over human life is a mission of the spirit, therefore man has to intensify his own spirituality. The machine can become, in human hands, a great asset for the conquest of the elements of nature on the sole condition that man himself becomes a free spirit. A wholesale process of dehumanization is going on and mechanicism is only the projection of this dehumanization. We can see this process in the dehumanizing of physical science. It studies invisible light-rays and inaudible sounds, and thereby leads man beyond the limits of his familiar world of light and sound; Einstein carries him beyond the world of space. These discoveries have a positive value and witness to the strength of human consciousness. Dehumanization is a spiritual state, the relation of the spirit to man and to the world.

Christianity liberated man from the bonds of the cosmic infinity that enslaved the ancient world, from the power of natural spirits and demons; it set him upright, strengthened him, made him dependent upon God and not upon Nature. But in the science which became accessible when man emancipated himself from Nature, on the heights of civilization and technique, he discovers the mysteries of cosmic life formerly hidden from him and the action of energies formerly dormant in the depths of Nature. This manifests his power, but it also places him in a precarious position in relation to the universe. His aptitude for organization disorganizes himself internally, and a new problem faces Christianity. Its answer to it presupposes a modification of Christian consciousness in the understanding of man's vocation in the world. The centre is in the Christian view of man as such, for we can no longer be satisfied by the patristic, scholastic, or humanistic anthropologies. From the point of view of cognition, a philosophical anthropology becomes a central problem: man and machine, man and organism, man and cosmos, are what it has to deal with. In working-out his historical destiny man traverses many different stages, and invariably his fate is a tragic one. At first he was the slave of Nature and valiantly fought for his own preservation, independence, and liberty. He created culture, states, national units, classes, only to become enslaved by his own creations. Now he is entering upon a new period and aims at conquering the irrational social forces; he establishes an organized society and a developed technique, but again becomes enslaved, this time by the machine into which society and himself are becoming transformed. In new and ever newer forms this problem of man's liberation, of his conquest of Nature and society, is being restated, and it can only be solved by a consciousness which will place him above them, the human soul above all natural and social forces. Everything that liberates man has to be accepted, and that which enslaves him rejected. This truth about man, his dignity and his calling, is embodied in Christianity, though maybe it has been insufficiently manifested in history and often even perverted. The way of man's final liberation and realization of his vocation is the way to the kingdom of God, which is not only that of Heaven but also the realm of the transfigured earth, the transfigured cosmos.

III

CHRISTIANITY AND HUMAN ACTIVITY

CHRISTIANITY AND HUMAN ACTIVITY

I

ALL existing arguments against Christianity are summarized in Soviet anti-religious literature. All that has been said by its opponents—Voltaire, Dupois, Feuerbach, Marx—is repeated, but in an exceedingly coarse and crude way. Even Lenin himself said nothing new about religion, though he surpassed all the others in coarseness and invective. Among all these arguments there is one central and even forcible one, which may sound plausible and perhaps convince those who are religiously ignorant and not given to seeking the core of religious problems: it is that every religion, and especially Christianity, rejects human activity. Religion on this hypothesis preaches passivity, submission to fate, humility in face of social injustice; it teaches man to lay the responsibility for all upon God, thereby justifying the oppression of man by man. In the Christian religion God alone is active; man has to remain passive: he may only pray and humble himself. All he can do is to order a *Te Deum* and wait for the outpouring of God's grace. In Soviet anti-religious literature this is generally illustrated by simple examples which contrast the fruitlessness of prayers and *Te Deums* for better crops, the expectation of miracles, with the good results following upon the use of better technical agricultural implements, with the improvement in the breed of horses resulting from the purchase of first-class brood-mares. The Tractor is presented to us in place of the former *Te Deum*. It is pointed out that religion counts on the backwardness, ignorance, and superstition of the religiously-minded masses, for whom Christianity, i.e. a religion of the spirit, has not yet been fully cut away from heathen magic. And Christians are forced to admit that too frequently in history Christianity has been interpreted as demanding man's servility and as rejecting his active and creative spirit. Theological treatises—Orthodox, Catholic, and Protestant—frequently abased and bore man down, denying his capacity for actively and creatively influencing his environment, Nature, and society, justifying only a conservative attitude towards life. Such an abasement of man, such a narrowing of the possibilities open to him, was generally related to the doctrine of man's sinful nature. He is a fallen being, original sin has undermined his strength; left to himself he can only produce what is bad: all that is good in his life proceeds from the grace of God. The teaching of Original Sin has been much misused. It has been made into a tool to enslave, to justify the injustice of life, to contend that sinful man can in no wise construct a righteous and free social life.

In order to understand the origin of this conception of Christianity and of the misuse of the doctrine of sinfulness we must keep in mind that the religious life of man is actuated by two principles, the divine and the human. The revelation of light, of light proceeding from God, has been given, but this revelation has been accepted by man with all his limitations. The social relations of men, their mutual mastery and servitude, have thrown their shadow upon this revelation. If God alone were active there would be no evil, no imperfection, no suffering: God's kingdom would be at hand. But man, too, is constantly active and this activity may be good, but it may also be bad. Man accepts the light proceeding from God in an active not in a passive spirit; its rays are refracted through his own darkness, they are perverted to suit his personal and social interests. He accepts God's revelation according to the standard of his own social status, and it is difficult for him to rise to a spiritual conception of Christianity. Man has often understood Christianity in a slavish way, and the very denial of man's creative power was engendered by a sinful spirit of human activity; the abasement of man was the evil human perversion of Christianity.

But Christianity in its pure unperverted essence speaks to us of the dignity of man; it elevates and never debases him. The very essence of the Gospel is the seeking for God's kingdom: "Seek ye first the kingdom of God"; it is the very core of Christianity. The Gospel says that "The kingdom of Heaven suffereth violence." Now to seek for the kingdom of God means to seek for perfect life, for the fullness of life, and everything that is true is part of that life. Seeking for the kingdom of God cannot include the service of evil and injustice resulting from human sinfulness. Sin is conquered by the most active seeking for God's kingdom, by the best, the most perfect, the fullest, the most complete life. We might truly say that "Christianity is an eternal revolutionary," because no order of life can ever satisfy it. It is seeking for the kingdom of God and for his truth—it is demanding the most radical transformation of man, society, and the world. Christianity differs from outward revolutionaries not because its ideas are less radical than theirs but because it demands that means and aims should correspond—it denies hatred and violence as a means for attaining perfect life. Christianity is no constant expectation of miracles, as something standing outside man and accomplished for him independently of his actual state. Such a passive expectation is condemned as a temptation. The possibility of the miraculous in human life presupposes human spiritual activity. Vladimir Soloviev once said that "It is impious to wait upon God to do that which simple justice could bring about." It is equally true that it is impious to expect God to give us better crops when human technical achievements can improve our agriculture. The same holds good for all the realms of our activity. God himself wants perfect life to be attained through human science and civilization, through medicine, through technical progress. But inner perfection of life, change of human souls, can be achieved by no science or technical improvements. It presupposes spiritual relations between man and God.

To assert that Christianity is hostile to man's activity contradicts, in the first place, history. The greatest possible human activity was manifested during the Christian epoch and the most dynamic development belongs to nations that have embraced Christianity—the nations of the West. It has proved itself to be a force building up and directing history. Even its foes were forced to admit that the nations of the ancient civilizations of the East—China, India, Persia—nations which refused to accept Christianity—fell out of step with the world's history: they stagnated, they lived in the past, they did not face the future. It was only Christianity that made nations capable of looking towards what was to come.

This can be explained by the messianic nature of Christianity, by the faith that the world was going forward to its definite, all-explaining goal—the kingdom of God. The very conception of history as a dynamic process, possessing a meaning of its own and advancing towards the highest aim, was created by Christianity. Such a conception became possible because, in the midst of history, Christ, the Saviour of the world, came into it, or in other words, the meaning of the world's processes was incarnated. The Greeks and the whole of ancient civilization had no true conception of history; their minds were not directed forward; they conceived the world as a revolving circle. The Greek was meditative, not active. He had an æsthetic love for the beauty of the cosmos, for the world's harmony; his religion was closely related to the myths of the past, and in this past the myths played an important part.

Christianity, on the other hand, lives not only in the past, but in the future as well. It is looking forward to the second coming of Christ, to the kingdom of God, to the end of the world, when the whole meaning of existence will be realized. The dynamism which was introduced by Christianity into the history of human societies is related to this seeking for God's kingdom—to the seeking for perfect life. Christianity alone knows aught of this intense seeking, this dissatisfaction with the existing world; it alone has implanted this anxiety in the soul. Man dares to be satisfied only with a perfection as complete as that of the Heavenly Father.

All the social utopias of the nineteenth century, all ideologies of a perfect social order, could become possible, even as ideas, only in a Christian world; all of them are transplanted into the social realm from the Christian idea of the kingdom of God. The idea of Karl Marx about the messianic mission of the proletariat is of religious origin, though it is rather the Judaic than the Christian conception that he adopts. The Greco-Roman civilization, aristocratic in its very principles, despised work and looked upon it as the portion of the slaves; it is only since Christianity, since the Gospel, that work and those who do it have been sanctified. Christ himself worked: "The labourer is worthy of his hire." The parables concerning the talents and the vineyard speak of human labour, of human activity, of human creative gifts: man must return his talents multiplied to God (Matt. xxv, 14-30; xxi, 28-31). The activity of man must be fruitful; he is told to till the soil; he must return increased all that he has received. Nowhere does the Gospel justify passivity. Christianity established the dignity of every man, 'fashioned in God's image and after his likeness,' and it opens an endless vista of perfection, a perfection not only of individuals but of social meaning. Christianity affirms that man is a spiritual being, and spirit is ever active; that is the definition of spirit. Matter is passive and inert. A spiritual being cannot but strive towards eternity, perfection, the fullness of life, and such a striving implies movement, dynamic development, activity. It was Christianity that set man free from the power of Nature, from the elemental forces in the midst of which ancient heathen man lived. In the pagan world man saw demons and spirits everywhere: he was afraid of them and felt that he was subject to them. Christianity released man from this dread of the chaos of dark demoniacal forces underlying Nature, it freed the human spirit from oppression; it raised man and subjected his fate to God, not to elemental natural forces, to the inner, not to the outward. Man could not learn to know Nature scientifically and conquer it technically so long as he thought it was peopled with spirits upon whom his own life depended. Christianity set man free from this pandemonism, thereby spiritually preparing the development of natural science and technical progress, the conquest of nature and its subjection to mankind.

But this did not become evident immediately. During the middle ages man had to pass through an ascetic and spiritual struggle against Nature, both within himself and outside. He had, first of all, to cut himself off from the Nature to which he had been subjected as a heathen. And yet the development of science and of technical progress in modern times became possible only thanks to the spiritual freedom which man had received in Christianity; these may rebel against Christianity, but they would not have been possible without the inner liberation of the human spirit which it entailed. Only a spirit which is raised above the world can conquer and subject the world: a spirit which is not merely an infinitesimal fraction of the world, a product and reflection of the world's processes, but one possessing another and inner source of strength. The world can be conquered only if the visible world surrounding and violating us from all sides is part of an invisible world in which we live and which is the source of our transfiguring creative energy. This is what Christianity teaches. But those who struggle against Christianity in the name of man's creative power think too superficially to notice, much less to understand, that it is so.

II

Let us look at the heart of the matter. What does Christianity teach us concerning man? Does it lower or raise him? At present we are interested not in the numerous perversions of historical Christianity or in the various ways in which it has been made to serve human interests: our purpose is to speak of its very essence in its all purity, in its inner hidden action on the human soul. Nowhere in Christian revelation, in the gospels, in the doctrines of the kingdom of God and of God having given his only Son for love of mankind and of the world, do we see aught that lowers man or diminishes his creative power. The Gospel demands that man should be active; that he should actively perfect himself; that he should serve his neighbour actively; that he should likewise actively seek the kingdom of God, which can be attained only "by violence."

All European humanism up to the period of its decline and decay, its teaching concerning the high dignity of man, the value of every human personality, and man's endless prerogatives, was of Christian origin. Christianity acted on the very depths of the human soul, transforming and transfiguring cruel, semi-animal, barbarian human nature (although subsequently man's mind was not loyal to religion and lost its faith). If this inner transformation had not taken place slavery would never have been overcome; there would never have been a declaration of the equality of man which is, above all, equality in the sight of God; freedom of human conscience and its independence of the State would never have been attained.

This, however, does not mean that the Christians of history, Christian governments, Christian bishops and clergy, have always struggled against slavery and been ready to abolish it. Sometimes they even defended it. But it does mean that Christianity transformed human feeling and appreciation inwardly, that it led to such an awakening and enlightening of the human conscience that slavery became intolerable. Even those who no more ranked themselves among the Christians profited in full by the results of the Christian regeneration of conscience. The greatest philosophers of antiquity,

Plato and Aristotle, could not rise to the conception which since Christianity is accessible even to the ordinary man. This does not mean that Christian authorities have always admitted liberty of conscience; frequently they rejected and crushed it; people were burnt at the stake for their religious convictions; it often happened that ecclesiastical customs abased man. But this does not impugn God's revelation through his Son, the true essence of Christianity. These abuses were the result of purely human conceptions arising from human limitations and human darkness, from man's having perverted Christian revelation to adapt it to his own human aims.

Yet, even so, it was Christianity alone that introduced true freedom of conscience. At the time of ancient civilization, in Greece and Rome, men were entirely dependent upon the State, the City: religion was a State religion, man possessed no inner spiritual freedom. In the Eastern monarchies man was a slave. Christianity was the first to establish man's spiritual independence from Nature and from the State: it set him before the face of God and denied the right of the State and of society to judge of his relations with God. The martyrs who refused to prostrate themselves before Cæsar spiritually won the battle for freedom of conscience. Perhaps some may rejoin that historical Christianity subordinated itself to the State, became its obedient servant, and when necessary used the temporal sword for its own interests; that it burnt heretics; that it established an inquisition which had been unknown in ancient Greece. But all these defections were the remnants of paganism in the midst of Christian humanity, human perversion of Christian truth traceable to the violence exercised by the State and by an unenlightened barbarous society against Christianity and the Christian conscience. Therefore when we speak of the part played by Christianity in history we must always keep in mind, not the actions of individual Christians or their governors or ecclesiastics, who were frequently unworthy of the name, but the inner influence of Christian consciousness on the human soul, on the emotional life of men, on their conscience.

Christian teaching regarding man is not limited to the fact that man is a fallen and sinful being and therefore powerless without aid from on high. In fact, this is not even the chief part of its teaching.

First of all, only he who stands can fall, and only a free spirit, not a slave of necessity, could fall away from God. Now the most important part of Christian teaching about man is that he is fashioned in the image and likeness of God. In man is reflected the highest nature; he is the creation of God, the child of God, and not merely a drop in the ocean of Nature's life: not a result of Nature's processes, and as such knowing naught of freedom. This higher nature of man as a free spirit could not have been destroyed and uprooted through original sin; the work of the Creator could not have been finally wiped out. As the image and likeness of God, man himself is a creator and is called to create. The book of Genesis teaches that man was created king over all created beings, organizer and tiller of the soil; it was he who had to give names to all the other beings. The very fact of his fall proves that he possessed power and freedom which could be directed both towards good and towards evil. But Christianity also teaches us that the Son of God, i.e. God himself, became man, took our human nature, thereby raising it to unutterable heights and opening to it the possibility of becoming divine. Through Christ, the God-man, man receives creative power which raises him above Nature.

In everyday "ordinary" Christianity, the religion of the average, unenlightened crowd, there are still many elements of superstition and remnants of heathen times; these take on a worse, a darker hue after the coming of Christ and in the midst of Christianity than they had in pagan times. Such a Christianity often oppresses and debases man, and turns him into a trembling, timorous creature.

Anti-religious propaganda finds its task all the easier because it frequently has to do with just such a Christianity and with its remnants of heathen superstition. That propaganda knows more of pagan magic than it does of true Christian mysticism.

Indeed, the representatives of this anti-religious propaganda evidently know nothing of any other kind of Christianity. But how different is the true faith, the religion of the God-man, of God and humanity, of the inner nearness of man to God. It presupposes not only belief in God but also belief in man, the possibility of uniting the divine and the human, the belief in God's having come down to man and of man being lifted up towards God.

Other historical religions, Judaism, Islam, Brahmanism, have believed in God. But Christianity, and Christianity alone, believes not only in God but in man as well, in manhood as potentially a reflection of the divine. This is the chief peculiarity of Christianity, its specific feature. It is the religion of the incarnation of the Spirit, of the transfiguration of the world; it is no rejection of the world and of mankind. Hindu religious consciousness rejects man and dissolves him in an impersonal divinity. Christianity asserts his dignity and wants to transform him and prepare him for eternity. The Church has rejected the quietism which taught that man was to be completely passive; she has also rejected the teaching which denied the activity implied in the idea of human freedom. Man can be active, victorious over the elemental forces of Nature and outside himself, the organizer and constructor of the world, only if he has within him the spiritual basis of life which raises him above Nature, only if he himself is no mere regeneration of Nature and of social environment—if the creative principle within him is independent of outward influence.

Now it is just the existence of such an inner spiritual principle that Christianity teaches, whereas materialism quite ignores it.

III

Can historical and philosophical materialism insist upon the existence of man's activity? Actually, the adherents of materialism do insist upon it, but in doing this do they remain true to their principles? Can they justify themselves logically?

Marxism teaches activity and its followers glorify it. But is the marxist teaching concerning man such as can justify human activity? Far from it. For the teaching that economic laws govern the whole of human life, that history unfolds itself according to the development of material productive forces, that every kind of ideology is only the reflection of existing economic conditions, is a passive teaching, leaving no room for the creative initiative of man. According to it, all that man does and all that he thinks is but the reflection of a material reality; man is pushed forward by impersonal material-social forces which lie outside his own being. This difficulty of justifying the activity of man according to the principles of Marx, especially the excessive activity of the Russian communists, produces the crisis of contemporary Soviet philosophy. Some attempts have been made to introduce certain corrections into the teaching of Marx, to set limits to his social determinism, to rise above a mechanical materialism, to admit the possibility of an independent, self-sufficing movement in the world, one that is not determined by environment. The young Russian communists want to build up a philosophy which will justify their activity,* but this can be achieved only by sacrificing logic and doing violence to the accepted terminology of philosophy. Matter is endowed by marxist philosophy with the freedom of spirit, with life, activity, logic, freedom, and the possibility of independent movement. But if we preserve the right terminology of philosophy we see that matter and material processes cannot be active, that free self-directed movement is not inherent in them, that no dialectical development can be theirs. Matter is inert and passive: spirit alone is active; activity presupposes a spiritual principle. If man is but an atom of the world's matter, the offspring and product of material nature and social environment, if he is but a passing moment and the tool of material, natural, and social processes, then there can be no question about man's activity. In such a world-view there can be no activity in the world at all, because

* See my essay: "The General Line of Soviet Philosophy" in *The End of Our Time* (Sheed and Ward, 1933).

all is determined from without; whatever is but the reflection of something else is the result of necessity. If the dialectical materialism of Marx and Lenin asserts an unheard-of activity of man as a social being, if it considers him able to transform the whole world according to his own ideas and even to set aside the laws of Nature, it is only because this teaching endows matter with qualities belonging only to spirit, thereby violating, as has already been said, the established terminology. Materialism is retained as an oral, conventional symbol, but it is rejected in fact.

Now we approach the main argument of anti-religious propaganda, what appears as the strongest attack against Christianity, and we shall at the same time see the chief refutation of this argument. The defence of the activity of man reveals itself as mere fiction. Those who accuse Christianity of denying man's activity themselves deny not only his activity, but deny even man himself.

The Soviet, Marx-Leninist, world-view asserts, *not the activity of man, but the activity of society or of a social collective body, which suppresses man and transforms him into its own instrument.* The activity of man implies that we acknowledge man's creative initiative and his freedom of action. Man is active if he is a free spiritual being, possessing an unconditional value, and not a simple instrument of social process; he is active if he creates this social process, not if the social process creates him. Soviet "activity" is no truly human activity, for man, each individual man, is only the obedient executor of a social command. Materialistic communism denies the very existence of man: the only elemental reality which it does admit is the social collective body, and this certainly is uncommonly active and powerful. If we wanted to borrow from Christian terminology, we might say that all activity proceeds from the "grace" of the collective body, from the Communist Party, and not from man's freedom. The collective body, the Communist Party, communist society, replace God.

Christianity is accused of considering God alone as active, and man as passive, i.e. of fatalism; God acts in the world independently of and not through man but, so to say, above him; he is no independent subject but just an object for divine activity: grace and not the freedom of man is the only active principle. But we know that the Catholic Church condemns "Occasionalism," i.e. the teaching according to which only the First Cause (God) acts in the world, whereas secondary causes, Nature and Man, are but motives for the activity of the First Cause. The Christian mind has always protested against a fatalistic conception of God's activity in the world: God works in the world not above, beyond, or aside from man, but *through* man, through his freedom and activity. If man were only the passive product of material Nature and society, the reflection of social processes, there would be much more reason to say that it is not in any way man which is acting, but only Nature and society, man himself being then but the passive instrument of the natural and social process.

The disciples of Marx and of Lenin may retort by declaring that Nature and society act through man's activity, through the lively struggle of classes, and protest against a fatalistic interpretation of Marxism. The latest Soviet philosophy has even refused to accept Marxism as a teaching of determinism and is ready to admit indeterminism, i.e. the freedom of matter itself: it condemns the mechanistic philosophy which rejects this activity of struggling men. But, then, let its exponents explain what reason they have that would justify them in interpreting Christianity in terms of such mechanistic philosophy. They presume that Christianity involves the belief that God acts upon men mechanically, as an outward shock, in the same manner in which the mechanistic theory explains the movement of matter. There is much more reason and foundation for understanding Christianity as the action of God and of God's grace through man's activity, by means of it, and not from above man and apart from him, acting from within on man's freedom, enlightening and strengthening it. At any rate, it is easier to picture that such relations exist between God and man, where relations are spiritual and free, than to imagine them existing between man and Nature and society materialistically conceived. Material relations always imply a certain outward violence. Only God, as a spiritual being, can act from within, on the depth of human conscience; he alone can act on human freedom and by means of it. Belief in God implies belief in this inward power which enlightens and strengthens human freedom.

The action of Nature and of society or of the central committee of the Communist Party on man in no wise implies freedom of the human spirit or its inward activity. Nature and society can do violence to man, they may force him to act in such and such a manner; and truly man constantly feels that Nature and environment are outraging him: he feels enslaved by the world of Nature and society. His activity is constantly only his adaptability to external demands and to social necessity, a protective adaptability. Creative activity, on the other hand, becomes apparent when man rises above the demands of his environment, when he is no longer transformed by it but transforms it.

Strictly speaking only that which proceeds from within merits the name of activity. If I toil from morning to night carrying out the compulsory orders of the dominating classes of the State, of the social collective body, or of the Central Committee, I remain passive. Labour may be passive. The work of slaves is passive, not only in the midst of a slave-owning society, but also in a capitalistic or a communist society. Of course man may be so perfectly drilled that he will *feel* free even in the midst of his slavery, *feel* active even in the midst of his passivity: he may be transformed into a disciplined social animal. But in such case he loses his true image as well as his dignity, and human society resembles an ant-hill. And sooner or later man will rebel, just as the down-trodden men in Dostoievsky's novels rebel. But the action of God upon man always implies freedom of spirit, the activity of man's spirit; such an action cannot be imagined as something outward or mechanical. God is a spirit, and he reacts upon man as upon a spiritual being. Spirit is freedom and activity. The slavery which we have so frequently found in the religious life not only of heathen but also of Christians always betokens an un-christian conception of religion; it is the reflection in Christianity of man's social slavery. Religious revelation was constantly perverted by the social slavery of men who received it in a slavish manner, and thus the action of God upon man was conceived as the action of any other natural or social power, and not as the action of spirit upon spirit. Society, especially society organized in a perfectly mechanical manner, may act on man from without and demand of him an activity useful for itself, at the same time leaving the inner man passive and enslaved. Examples of oppression and tyranny which are so plentiful in the history of Christianity were always the oppression and tyranny, not of God, not of spirit, but of human society organized according to the pattern of dominion and subjection and only hiding behind Christian symbols, signs, and formulas.

An analogy was sometimes made between God and state authority; he was represented as an autocratic monarch and the Church as a monarchy: social relations and connections were carried over into religious life. Here much can be explained in the way that Marx explains it, by historical materialism. But what does this prove? It only means that whatever was slavish and rejected the activity of man in religious life, in Christianity itself, was not of religious but of social origin; it was a limitation and a perversion of spirit by society and by Nature, which aspects alone are accepted as realities by those who conduct anti-religious propaganda. They deny the spirit, the only source of activity and freedom, man's highest dignity, and they accept as supreme realities Nature and society, which are the true sources of passivity and slavery. They belong to the same category as the pseudo-Christians who in the past perverted Christian revelation. The activity of men is founded on the principle that the spirit is victorious over Nature and society; then only do the relations of man with them become free, freely active. Thus the principal argument of anti-religious propaganda not only falls to pieces, but is turned against the very people who put it forward. Those who struggle for man's activity must fight for spirit and against the unlimited outward domination of society.

IV

It is not Christianity in its true purity that rejects human activity: it is materialistic communism, Marxism, which does so. In such a materialistic world-view man is the object, not the subject; and this means that man is not active, for only the subject can act. If man is only the object for society's activity, a medium for social influence and demands, it becomes a mystery wherein consists the active element in him, i.e. the inner element, not the one engrafted from outside. His activity as affirmed by social materialism is that of a perfect automaton. He is transformed into a continually working machine which is set in motion by social organs; he is emptied of his inner kernel, his free spiritual being, of all that makes him a man; he cannot and dare not act of his own will, following the dictates of his inner self; he can and must act only because he is wound up from outside by society, by the social collective body, by the central committee of the Party, etc. It is ridiculous to read the accusation in Soviet writings against Christianity that it rejects man's activity and degrades him. For it is not man that the Soviet world-view sets upon a pinnacle but a machine, an improved social automaton; it is that that is declared to be active, extraordinarily and thunderously active. This automatic machine is set to work by the central organs of the social collective body; man is only the means and the instrument. Certainly, man has been called to work, he cannot remain wholly contemplative, but it is possible to have also a false, a senseless activity, one that leaves him no time free to think, scarcely to breathe, which makes every moment of his life only a preparation for the next one, destroys him, destroys his inner life, kills his soul. Man belongs not only to time but to eternity, and it is from eternity, from his spiritual source, that he draws strength for activity in the temporal world. Activity is a function of man and not man a function of activity. What can be said of that human activity which looks upon him as simply a means to social activity, a perfected machine, not made to serve the end, but the end subjected to the means? Those who wish to see the final mechanization and rationalization of human life can have nothing to say of true human activity. False activity rejects the value of man himself; it subjects him to the stream of time and destroys eternity. But he can work actively only if he is a spiritual being, and he is a spiritual being only if he belongs to eternity, if the eternal principle, independent of time, is not dead within him. And this is just what Christianity teaches; Christianity—but not Marxism or materialism.

A great Christian philosopher of the end of the

nineteenth century, N. F. Fedorov, who has not been sufficiently appreciated, especially insisted upon the activity of man. He believed that man was called to conquer the forces of Nature, to become master over space, to be victorious over death. The objectives which he set before man were much grander than those proposed by the Marx-Leninists, who are quite willing to submit passively to the most dreaded of all evils, the victory of death. Fedorov, whose *Philosophy of the Common Work* is formally somewhat similar to the teaching of Marx and Lenin though it is quite opposed to its spirit and final aim, could believe in a hitherto unheard-of activity of man because he believed in man. And this faith in man he received from Christianity, not from an outward perverted form but from an inner pure Christianity. If Fedorov had been a materialist such a belief in the activity of man would have been foolishness. His activity has to be revealed and justified in a whole and regenerated Christianity, and this is what Fedorov does. The Marx-Leninists contrast the passivity and inertia of Christianity with the remarkable industry of their reconstruction of life, their industrialization, their five-year plan. Certainly one cannot deny the capacity for action found in the Soviet younger generation, or its longing for work. Lenin once said that his chief aim was to conquer the "Oblomov" in every Russian,* and pro-

* "Oblomov," hero of one of Gonthkarov's novels. An example of a man frittering away his life in planning much but doing nothing.

bably one of the best positive results of the revolution will be the disappearance of "Oblomovs," the victory over the old Russian sloth. But Oblomov and Christianity have nothing in common; he was a very poor Christian. It is not Christianity which is to blame, but a Russian national characteristic fostered by serfdom. The Orthodox builders of the Russian Empire, whatever our appreciation of their work, cannot be reproached with an "Oblomov" sloth: that was the product of the aristocratic idleness of the epoch of Peter the Great.

But to return to the activity of the young generation in Soviet Russia. First of all, it admits of only one kind of activity: an economic-technical activity—for economic and technical values are the only true values and the whole process of life is subjected to them. This means the industrialization of the country according to the five-year plan (*Piatiletka*), which for them is blended with socialistic construction. Nothing else counts. All other branches of human creative activity are rejected, or narrowed down and subjected to economic and technical aims. Activity is reduced to pure mechanization, to machinery, to technical progress in everyday life.

But such results of activity have a sinister side. They react on the active subject, on man, who himself becomes a mechanism, an automaton, an obedient social animal. Outwardly he is remarkably active, but inwardly he is passive and obedient; he only carries out the orders received from the centre. Even in philosophy the directions given by the leaders of the Communist Party must be carried out by the young worker; in the realm of abstract thought they must spread the idea of socialistic construction as laid down by the five-year plan. The same holds true for literature and art. Everywhere they must carry out the orders for socialistic work, the thought and creative impulse of man must become the servants of the socialist collective body. Outward activity is related to inward passivity, to the passive obedience of will and thought. Man's spirit not only dare not be active or have creative initiative, but it must be reduced to a state of complete passivity; it must be simply extinguished: then only can the maximum of outward activity be attained.

This is what is achieved by the rationalization of human life. Such a rationalization is, of course, the result of unprecedented activity, but it is the activity of the automaton and of the machine, not of the human spirit; whereas the activity accepted by Christianity is, above all, activity of the human spirit; the machine must be subjected to the spirit and become its tool.

When our contemporaries, especially the young communist generation, speak of activity, of constructive work, they take it for granted that only one kind merits recognition—that which is technical and economic. It is not only the Russian communists who think so: European and American bourgeois capitalists are of the same opinion. Such a mentality belongs to a soulless technical epoch, when the aims of life have become dim and man is engrossed in the pursuit of the means of existence. Why, then, can a change in the relations of man to man, a change that will render these relations more human and generous, not be considered as an activity, as the realization of a new and better life? Why is such a realization not a spiritual activity, transforming man himself, enlightening his whole being? At present, activity and realization are related only to the search for the means of life; they have nothing to do with its aims and meaning.

Idolatry exists in Soviet Russia: a bowing-down before technical achievement, a superstitious veneration for machines. Such an attitude is easier in a technically backward country, where progress in this domain seems new and wonderful. Lenin's cry, "The electrification of all Russia," seemed to the people something very bold, daring, and revolutionary; the "miracles" of technical skill must verily appear miraculous in a literal sense to the Russians and their attitude towards them is almost one of religious worship. They seem to them to be akin to magic, and truly technical achievements are often the development of what was formerly considered magic. In fact, magic and technical progress have a single aim: the conquest of Nature.

Ridiculing miracles is one of the most established methods of anti-religious propaganda; the expectation of miracles, the prayer for miracles, are identified with the rejection of human activity, with the passivity and abasement of man: the miracles of technical progress must be victorious over God's miracles. But from the religious point of view a miracle must not be understood as something passive; it is not something that happens to man while he remains inert: that is a superstitious attitude. A miracle takes place with the active co-operation of man, it happens only to those who are worthy of it, who have merited it by their spiritual activity. A miracle is no denial or rejection of the laws of Nature; it acts through her powers and with their aid. But at the same time it is the revelation of a new spiritual power which surpasses the limited system of natural forces. The denial of miracles on principle can be founded only on the surmise that Nature is completely rounded off and finally organized, a system of forces acting in a hermetically closed sphere.

This is quite an arbitrary surmise. In actual fact the system of nature as revealed to the experience of our senses is part of an endless vista; new forces may pour into it, quite changing the results of the existing mutual reactions of forces. A miracle is a relative conception; it may be but the active intervention into the system of a new spiritually stronger force;

what we call the miraculous cure of a sick man is the revelation of a spiritual force that has conquered the destructive forces of Nature. It is foolish to point to technical achievements in order to contrast them with miracles: the two belong to different categories. Technical progress is no revelation of new forces but only a combination of existing natural forces which have been adapted and made obedient to the practical aims of man.

We must not shrink from the truth. We must admit that there is something in what Marx and Marxists say about religion and Christianity. Class-greed and class-falsehood have been mixed up with the religious life of human societies. Religion has often been used to justify the oppression of man by man. But the truth about the wrongs of religion must be wholly attributed to the outward, social side of religious life, which is the only side that counts with the Marxists. In fact, Marx-Leninists never apprehend true religion, they only see the politics which have distorted religion. This imperception derives from their initial point of view. They are incapable of looking into the depths, into the inner spiritual life, because for them life is on the surface and they see only the superficial side of things. All the attempts they make to prove from the point of view of historical materialism that the Gospel and Christ himself taught class-exploitation and class-oppression produce a pitifully unconvincing impression. But, to tell the truth, they do not greatly insist upon them—they generally prefer to put forward instances of historical human abuses and perversions of Christian truth. This is a much easier task. Beyond doubt the Christian life of human societies also reflects the social relations of dominion and subjection, of social oppression, the enslavement of man; but this has no relation to Christian truth and revelation, which have a spiritual, not a social source: they are the outpouring of spiritual forces on to our social-natural world. The denial of human activity by Christians was only the expression of man's sinful despondency, of human fear and slavery.

But the essence and meaning of Christianity is that it sets man free from despondency, fear, and slavery. In doing this Christianity liberates the creative activity of man, re-establishes his lost dignity. Man is called to act in the midst of society; but he can manifest his activity, dominate his social environment, subject his social relations and make them serve spiritual ends, only if his activity is not blind obedience to the commands of that same environment and those social relations but an answer to the call of a deeper, inner, spiritual power. In order to be able to act, he must begin by clearly establishing which are the highest value, aim, and meaning of his life, and he cannot gain a true understanding of them from his environment, either social or natural, for it is to them that he has to impart this value, aim, and meaning. Christianity teaches us *wherein* lies their highest eternal source, thereby spiritually raising man to a higher level than that of his environment: he can no longer be enslaved by it. It becomes possible for him to change, improve, and transfigure this environment, to subject it to the human spirit, to realize within it the highest value and meaning. More important still, Christianity gives a meaning and value to the personal existence of man.

This is something that no merely social teaching can do.

IV

THE WORTH OF CHRISTIANITY AND THE UNWORTHINESS OF CHRISTIANS

THE WORTH OF CHRISTIANITY AND THE UNWORTHINESS OF CHRISTIANS

I

BOCCACCIO tells the story of a Jew whose Christian friend was trying to convert him. The Jew was on the point of agreeing, but before committing himself definitely he decided to go to Rome and see for himself in what manner the Pope and his cardinals lived, since they were the men at the head of the Church. This frightened the Christian, who thought that all his efforts would go for nothing and his friend certainly refuse baptism when he had seen the scandals of Rome. The Jew duly went there and observed the hypocrisy, depravity, corruption, and greed which were rife among the Roman clergy and in the papal court at that time, and on his return his Christian friend asked anxiously what impression had been made on him. The reply was as deeply understanding as it was unexpected: "Since all the wickedness and abominations that I have seen in Rome have been unable to overturn the Christian religion, since in spite of them all it continues to grow stronger, it must be the true faith." And the Jew became a Christian

Whatever Boccaccio's idea may have been, this tale shows us the only way of vindicating Christianity. Christians themselves are the greatest objection to their religion; they are a scandal to those who are favourably disposed towards it. This argument has been grievously abused in our day. The present weakness of faith and spread of complete unbelief lead men to judge Christianity by Christians; formerly it was judged in the first place by its eternal truth, its doctrinal and moral teaching. Our age is too preoccupied with man and what is human, so that Christianity is not seen behind its mask of bad Christians; notice is taken of their wrongdoing and their deformations of the faith rather than of the religion itself; their excesses are more easily seen than the great Christian truth. Very many people to-day estimate the Christian religion by those whose profession of it is exterior and degenerate: Christianity is the religion of love and of freedom, but it is judged according to the hostility and hate and acts of violence of so many Christians, men who compromise their faith and are a stumbling-block to the weak.

We are often told that the representatives of other religions, Buddhists, Mohammedans, Jews, are better than Christians in that they are more faithful to their religious precepts; unbelievers, atheists, and materialists are pointed out who are more worthy of respect, more unworldly in their lives, more capable of sacrifice than are many Christians. But the whole of the unworthiness of these numerous Christians resides exactly in that they do not fulfil their religion, but rather alter and pervert it. They are judged by their inability to raise themselves to the heights of that which they profess. But how then can the shortcomings of Christians he imputed to Christianity when the reproach levelled at them is precisely that they are out of accord with the grandeur of their faith? These charges are clearly contradictory. If the followers of other religions are often more observant of them than Christians are of theirs, it is because these religions are more within the reach of man than are the heights of Christianity. It is indeed much more easy to be a good Mohammedan than a good Christian. The religion of love is not less exalted or less true because its realization in life is an exceedingly difficult task. It is not Christ's fault that his truth is not fulfilled and that his commandments are spurned.

Believing and practising Jews are always ready to tell us that the law of their religion has the great advantage of being practicable; Judaism is more adapted to human nature and to the ends of human life and calls for less renunciation. Christianity, on the other hand, is the most difficult religion to put into practice, the most trying to human nature, requiring painful self-sacrifice at every turn; Jews look on it as an idealistic dream, useless in practical life and for that reason harmful. We too often measure the moral value of men by their religion and ideals. If a materialist is good according to his light, devoted to his idea and ready to make certain sacrifices for it, then we are impressed by his greatness of soul and cite him as an example. But it is infinitely harder for a Christian to keep abreast of his ideal, for it means that he has got to love his enemies, carry his cross bravely, and resist the temptations of the world unflinchingly—things which neither the Jew nor the Mohammedan nor the materialist is called on to do. Christianity takes us along the line of greatest resistance, the Christian life is a crucifixion of self.

II

It is often claimed that Christianity has failed, that it has not been historically realized, and thence another argument is drawn : Not only Christians but the very history of their Church testifies against it. It must be recognized that the reading of ecclesiastical history can be an occasion of scandal to those whose faith is unsteady. These books tell us of the conflict within the Christian world, of human passions and temporal interests, of the corruption and disfigurement of truth in the consciousness of sinful mankind; very often they show periods of church-history which remarkably resemble those of civil governments, with their diplomatic relations, wars, and so on.

The outward history of the Church is visible and can be set out so that it is accessible to all. But her inward and spiritual history, the turning of men to God, the development of holiness, cannot be seen so easily; it is more difficult to write about them because they are in a way obscured and sometimes even overwhelmed by exterior history. Men detect evil more easily than good, they are more conscious of the outer than of the inner aspect of life; we have no difficulty in learning about the externals of our fellows, their commercial undertakings, their politics, their domestic and social institutions. But do we think much about the way in which men pray to God, how they relate their inner life to the divine world, in what manner they war spiritually with temptation?

Very often we know nothing, do not even suspect the existence, of a spiritual side to those whom we meet—at the most we are conscious of it only in those whom we know particularly well. We are quick to note the exterior manifestations of evil passions that anyone can see, but as for what lies behind them, the spiritual struggles, the reachings-out to God, the toilsome endeavours to live the truth of Christ—we do not know them, we may even not want to know them. We are told not to judge our neighbour, but we judge him continually, by his outward actions, by the expression of his face, without ever looking within.

It is just the same with the history of Christianity. It cannot be judged by external facts, by the human passions and human sins that disfigure its image. We have got to recall to our minds what Christian people have had to contend with in the course of ages and their bitter struggles to get the better of "the old man," of their ancestral heathenism, of their age-long barbarity, of their grosser instincts; Christianity has had to work its way through the matter which put up such a solid resistance to the spirit of Christ, it has had to raise up to a religion of love those whose appetites were all for violence and cruelty. Christianity is here to heal the sick not the whole, to call sinners not the righteous, and mankind, converted to Christianity, is sick and sinful. It is not the business of the Church of Christ to organize the external part of life, to overcome evil by material force; she looks for an inner and spiritual rebirth from the reciprocal action of human freedom and divine grace. It is an essential quality of Christianity that it cannot get rid of self-will, the evil in human nature, for it recognizes and respects the freedom of man.

Materialistic socialists are given to proclaiming that Christianity is not a success, that it has not made the kingdom of God actual; it is nearly two thousand years since the Redeemer of the world appeared on earth and evil still exists, it even increases: the world is saturated with suffering and the burdens of life are no less for all that our salvation has been accomplished. These socialists promise to do, without God and without Christ, what Christ himself could not bring about: the brotherhood of man, justice in social life, peace, the kingdom of God on earth—these unbelievers willingly use that expression, "the kingdom of God on earth"!

The only experience that we have of materialistic Socialism in practice is the Russian experiment, and that has not given the expected results. But there is no solution of the question in it. Socialism's promise to make justice rule on earth and to get rid of evil and suffering does not rest on human freedom but on the violation of it; its ends are to be realized by an enforced social organization which shall make external evil impossible by compelling men to virtue, righteousness, and justice—and it is this constraint that constitutes the great difference between Socialism and Christianity. The so-called "failure of Christianity in history" is a failure dependent upon human freedom, upon resistance springing from our Christ-given freedom, upon opposition by the ill will which religion will not *compel* to be good. Christian truth supposes freedom, and looks to an interior and spiritual victory over evil. Exteriorly the State can set a limit to the manifestations of wickedness and it is its duty to do so, but evil and sin will not be overcome in that way. There is no such dilemma for the socialist, because he knows no problem of sin or of the spiritual life; the only question facing him is that of suffering and social injustice and their elimination by means of an organization of life from without. God does not use force, for he desires man's freedom and not merely an exterior triumph of righteousness. In that sense it may be said that he maintains evil and uses it for good ends. In particular, the righteousness of Christ cannot be actualized by force. But the justice of Communism is to be attained by compulsion, and this can be done the more easily because any freedom of spirit is denied.

The argument based on a historical defeat of Christianity cannot be sustained. The kingdom of God cannot be imposed; if it is to be brought about we must be born again, and that supposes complete freedom of spirit. Christianity is the religion of the Cross, and it sees a meaning in suffering. Christ asks us to take up our own cross and carry it, to shoulder the load of a sinful world. In Christian consciousness the notion of attaining happiness, justice, and the kingdom of God on earth without cross or suffering is a huge lie: it is the temptation that Christ rejected in the wilderness when he was shown the kingdoms of the world and invited to fall down and worship. Christianity does not promise its own necessary realization and victory here below; Christ even questioned whether he will find any faith on earth when he comes again at the end of time, and foretold that love itself will have grown cold.

Tolstoy believed that Christ's commands could be easily fulfilled simply by recognizing their truth. But that was a mistake of his over-rationalizing consciousness; the mysteries of freedom and of grace were beyond him, his optimism contradicted the tragic depths of life. "The good which I will I do not," says the apostle Paul, "but the evil which I will not, that I do. Now if I do that which I will not it is no more I that do it, but sin that dwelleth in me." This testimony of one of the greatest of all Christians unveils the innermost part of the human heart, and it teaches us that the "failure of Christianity" is a human failure and not a divine defeat.

III

In the course of history there has been a triple betrayal of Christianity by Christendom. Christians first of all deformed their religion, then separated themselves from it, and finally—and this was the worst wrong of all—began to blame it for the evils which they had themselves created. When Christianity is adversely criticized it is the sins and vices of Christian men and women that are criticized, their non-application and perversion of Christ's truth, and it is to a great extent because of these human perversions, sins, and wickednesses that the world abandons the faith.

Man perverts Christianity in some respect and then turns upon both the perversion and the real thing; the matters of which the detractors of Christianity complain cannot be found in the words of Christ, in his precepts, in the holy Scriptures, in sacred Tradition, in the Church's teaching, or in the lives of the saints. An ideal principle must be opposed by another, an actual fact must be met with another actual fact. It is possible to defend the cause of Communism by showing that it has been perverted and never properly applied, just as can be done for Christianity. Communists shed blood and denaturalize truth to gain their ends just as Christians have done, but to assimilate the two systems one to the other in consequence of this would be an obvious fallacy.

In the gospels, in the words of Christ, in the teaching of the Church, in the example of the saints, and in other perfect manifestations of Christianity, there can be found the good news of the coming of God's kingdom, calls to love of one's neighbour, to gentleness, to self-denial, to cleanness of heart; but nothing can be found there in favour of violence, hostility, revenge, hate, or greed. On the other hand, in the ideology of Marx, which is the breath of Communism, you *can* find appeals to revenge, to the malicious animosity of one class for another, to the war for personal interests, but nothing at all about love, sacrifice, forbearance, or spiritual purity. Christians have often committed these crimes and professedly under the banner of Christ, but in so doing they have never been fulfilling his commandments. Our adversaries delight in saying that Christians have often resorted to force for the defence or spreading of their religion. The fact is inconstestable; but it only shows that these men were blinded by passion, that they were still unenlightened, that their sinfulness perverted the most righteous and sacred cause, that they did not understand of what spirit they were. When Peter drew his sword in defence of Jesus and smote off the ear of the high priest's servant, Jesus said to him: "Put up again thy sword into its sheath, for all that take the sword shall perish by the sword."

The Christian revelation and religious life, like all revelation and all religious life, suppose the existence of man as well as the existence of God. And man, although enlightened by the light of grace which comes from God, accommodates this divine light to the eye of his own spirit and imposes on revelation the limitations of his own nature and consciousness.

We know from the Bible that God revealed himself to the Jews. But he was more than the wrathful, jealous, and avenging God reflected in the consciousness of the Jewish people. Men limited Christian truth too, and deformed it as well. Thus God was often represented as some eastern potentate, an arbitary monarch, and the dogma of the Redemption was interpreted as the cessation of his judicial proceedings, begun because he was aggrieved against mankind, the transgressor of his will. It was this perverted understanding and human limiting of its doctrines that led men to give up Christianity. Even the idea of the Church was spoiled. It was made solely an external thing, solely identified with a hierarchy, with ceremonial observances, with the transgressions of "parochial Christian," and it was looked on first, foremost, and above all as an institution. The deeper and more inward understanding of the Church as a spiritual organism, the mystical body of Christ (as St. Paul defines it), was forced almost out of sight and became accessible only to the few. The liturgy and the sacraments were treated only as external rites, for their profound and hidden meaning completely escaped these pseudo-Christians. And so people left the Church, shocked by the vices of the clergy, by the mistakes of ecclesiastical organizations, by a too close likeness to a government department, by the hypocritical sham piety or the too ostentatious devoutness of the rank-and-file.

It must always be remembered that the life of the Church is theandric, there is a divine element and a human element, and these elements interact. Her foundation is eternal and infallible, sacred and sinless, it cannot be altered, and the gates of hell shall not prevail against it. The divine element in the Church is Christ, her head, the fundamental structure of our religion, the dogmas of divine revelation, the evangelical moral teaching, the sacraments, the action of the grace of the Holy Spirit. But on the human side the Church is fallible and subject to change: there can be deformation, disease, failure, alteration, just as there can be creative activity, development, enrichment, rebirth. The sins neither of mankind in general nor of the ecclesiastical hierarchy in particular are the sins of the Church taken in her divine essence and they do not lessen her holiness. Christianity requires that human nature be enlightened and transfigured: human nature resists and tends to pervert its religion. In the continuous tension between the two elements sometimes the one is in the ascendant, sometimes the other.

Christianity raises man and sets him at the centre of the universe. The Son of God took on our flesh and by so doing sanctified our nature. The Christian religion points out to man the highest aim in life and appeals to his exalted origin and great mission. But, unlike other religions, it does not flatter human nature: it calls on man heroically to overcome his fallen and sinful state.

Human nature, undermined by original sin, is but little receptive: it cannot contain the divine truth of Christianity and has difficulty in grasping the theandric notion involved in the coming of Christ, God-man. He teaches us to love God and to love man, our neighbour, and the love of the one and the other are indissolubly bound together. We love our brethren through God, through the Father, and by our love for them we evince our love for God. "If we love one another God abideth in us and his charity is perfected in us." Christ was both Son of God and Son of man and he revealed to us the perfect union of God and man, the humanity of God and the divinity of man. But the natural man finds this fulness of a divine and human love difficult in practice. Sometimes he veers towards God and away from man, ready for divine love but indifferent and cruel to his fellows: it was thus in the Middle Ages. At other times he is all agog to love and serve man but without reference to God, even opposing the very idea of him as mischievous and contrary to the good of mankind: it is thus in the new age, with its Humanism and humanitarian Socialism. Then, when they have rejected the theandric truth and disassociated love of man from love of God, people proceed to attack Christianity and arraign it for their own misdeeds.

IV

The intolerance, fanaticism, and cruelty that Christians have so often displayed are products of the difficulty, to which I have referred, that human nature finds in containing the fulness of Christian truth, its love and freedom. Men assimilate a part of the truth and are content with that; the full light reaches only a few. Man has a capacity for perverting anything, even absolute truth, and turning it into an instrument to serve his own passions. The very apostles themselves, the companions of Christ in the flesh, enlightened directly by him, understood his truth only in part and in too human a way, adapting it to their limited Jewish ideas.

To reproach the Christian religion for the fires of the Inquisition and the fanaticism, intolerance, and cruelty of the Middle Ages is to tackle the problem the wrong way round. An attack on medieval religion, founded on a statement of indisputable (but sometimes exaggerated) facts, is not an attack upon Christianity but upon people: it is man attacking man. The theocratic principle was proper to medieval Catholicism; in virtue of it the Church was considered over-much as a State, and some even conferred on the Pope a sovereignty over the whole world. But it was the barbarous nature of man, not the Catholic Church, that was responsible for the accompanying cruelty and intolerance. The world at that era was shot through with violent and bloody instincts, and the Church set herself to organize, tame, and christianize this anarchically-inclined world. The resistance of unenlightened human nature was so strong that she did not always succeed; the medieval world may be regarded as formally Christian but it was in essence half-Christian, half-pagan, and the ecclesiastical hierarchy itself was often enough sinful, bringing ambition and other human passions into the life of the Church and so disfiguring the truth of Christ. But the divine element continued intact and enlightening; the evangelical voice of our Lord was always there to be heard in its unalloyed purity. Had it not been for the Christian Church the world of the Middle Ages would have been drowned in blood, and spiritual culture would have perished altogether in Europe, for the best achievements of the culture of Greco-Roman antiquity were conserved by her and handed on to succeeding ages. The scholars, philosophers, and "intellectuals" of those days were all monks, and it is Christianity we have to thank for the type of chivalric knight, who made rude vigour gentle and its rough strength noble. And anyway, the natural ferocity of medieval man was sometimes better than the mechanization of his contemporary descendant.

Fanaticism did not so much characterize the Eastern Orthodox Church, which knew no Inquisition or similar violences in questions of religion and conscience. Her historical faults were due to a too great submission to the civil power.

There were human perversion and sin both in the Catholic Church and in the Orthodox Church, but the errors of Christianity as practised in the world were always the errors of individual Christians, arising from their natural weakness. If we do not live according to unsullied truth it is we who are to blame, not truth.

Men require freedom and are not willing to be constrained to goodness. Nevertheless, they charge God with the consequences of the unlimited freedom that he has given them.

Is either Christ or Christianity responsible for the fact that human life is full of evil?

Christ never taught the things that people criticize and repudiate in Christianity; if we had followed his precepts there would have been no reason for revolt against his religion.

In one of H. G. Wells's books there is a dialogue between men and God. The men complain that life is full of wickedness and suffering, wars, excesses of all sorts, so that it becomes unbearable, and God replies: "If you don't like these things, don't do them." This remarkably simple passage is very instructive. Christianity on earth has to operate in a land of darkness, surrounded by the forces of wickedness, both natural and supernatural; the might of Hell is arrayed against Christ and his Church. These evil powers are at work inside as well as outside the Church and Christianity, seeking to corrupt the one and change the other; but though the abomination of desolation is set up in the holy place this none the less remains holy, and even shines more brilliantly. Those who have spiritual sight see perfectly clearly that to pervert Christianity and then blame it for that for which it is not responsible is to crucify Christ anew. He gives his blood eternally for the sins of the world, for those who deny and crucify him.

Truth cannot be gauged by the behaviour of men, especially of the worst of them. Truth must be looked in the face and seen by its own light, and among the human reflections of that truth judgement must be made according to the best of them; the Christian religion must be judged by its apostles and martyrs, by its heroes and saints, and not by the mass of half-Christian-half-pagans who do all they can to deform the image of their faith.

Two greats tests were given to Christian mankind, persecution and victory. The first was surmounted, and by its martyrs and confessors under the Romans Christianity triumphed in its beginnings as it does under communist persecution in Russia to-day. But the test of victory is harder, and when the Emperor Constantine bowed down before the Cross and Christianity became the official religion of the

Empire there began a very long test of that kind. And it was surmounted less successfully than the other. Christians often changed from persecuted into persecutors, they let themselves succumb to the temptations of the kingdoms of this world and their power; it was then that there crept into Christianity those perversions of its truth that have been made the source of accusations against it. Christianity is not responsible for that which its critics do not understand, the joy of earthly victory. Christ was crucified once more, for those who looked on themselves as his servants while they did not know of what Spirit they were.

V

The men of to-day who are so far from Christianity are fond of saying that the Church ought to be made up of perfect people, saints, and complain of her that she includes so many faulty persons, sinners, and pseudo-Christians. It is the standing argument against Christianity, and it is one that betrays non-comprehension or forgetfulness of the nature and essence of the Church. The Church exists before all else for sinners, for imperfect and wandering beings. Her origins are in Heaven and her principle is eternal, but she operates on the earth and in time, among elements submerged in sin; her first business is to succour an erring world at grips with suffering, to save it for eternal life and raise it to the heavens. The essence of Christianity is a union of eternity and time, of Heaven and earth, of the divine and the human, and *not* any separation between them: the human and temporal are not to be despised and rejected but enlightened and transfigured.

In the early days of Christianity there was a sectarian movement called Montanism, which claimed that the Church ought to consist exclusively of righteous and godly beings and that all others should be rejected by her; she was for the Montanists a community of those who had received special gifts from the Holy Spirit and by far the greater part of mankind, being sinful, was to be completely repudiated by her. Ecclesiastical consciousness condemned Montanism and upheld the Church as the home of sinners who repent. The saints are the Church's bulwark and buttress, but she does not depend on them alone, for the whole of mankind, a mankind seeking salvation, contributes in varying degrees to her perfecting. The Church on earth is the Church Militant warring with evil and iniquity, she is not yet the Church Glorified. Christ himself consorted with publicans and sinners, and the Pharisees criticized him for it. His Church has to be like him. A Christianity that extended its recognition only to good people would be a pharisaical Christianity. Compassion, forgiveness, charity towards one's neighbour with all his shortcomings are the work of Christian love and the means towards its perfection. To accuse Christianity of the shadow which darkens the destiny of the Church is a product of pharisaism.

Montanism is an example of false maximizing; it is spiritual pride, false morality, lack of love. The falsehood of maximizing consists in requiring the most from others but not from oneself, we accuse them of not achieving a perfection of goodness that we have not thought of attempting. Those who have reached holiness are not in the habit of accusing others. Christianity, the religion of love, unites austerity, strictness, exactingness towards self with sympathy, charity, and gentleness towards one's neighbour. The charges of our contemporaries are only pretexts for their animosity against Christianity, attempted justifications of their own treachery towards it: they shelter behind a false morality.

Christianity must not be confused with Tolstoyism, which is an abstract moralism. Tolstoy criticizes the historical so-called Christianity radically and cruelly, and his criticism is not without justification, for it is founded on facts. He claims that the Christian religion was professed as an abstraction, without any actualization of it in life and conduct. For him our Lord's moral teaching constituted the whole of the Christian religion: he was ignorant of or opposed to its hidden mystical sides. He believed that everything depends on the truth of a concept, and that once it is conceived it is a simple matter to put it into practice; if one recognizes the veritable law of the master of life, that is, of God, it will be easy, by virtue of that recognition, to actualize it. Tolstoy did not recognize man's freedom or see the evil lurking in the depths of human nature: he imagined the source of wickedness to be in the consciousness instead of in the will and its freedom. Accordingly he did not have recourse to the help of divine grace for the overcoming of evil but looked to a modification of consciousness. Jesus Christ was for him not a saviour and redeemer but a great educator for life, a moral legislator, and Tolstoy thought Christianity easy of realization because it is simpler, more advantageous, and wiser to live according to a law of love than according to the law of hatred favoured by the world. He had an idea that Christ teaches us "not to do silly things." He attributed the blame for the fact that the religion of Christ is not made real in life to theological teaching which concentrates attention on our Lord himself, building up all things on the redemption accomplished by him and on divine grace. Tolstoy attacked the Church at her foundations.

He was right to demand that Christianity be taken seriously and that Christ's precepts be translated into action, but he was mistaken in believing that this is easy and that it can be done simply by means of an enlightened consciousness, without Christ our

Saviour or the grace of the Holy Spirit. In asking men to make this attempt Tolstoy fell into the error of moral maximizing. For the rest, he did not succeed in realizing in his own life the doctrine that he upheld. The only Christianity that he recognized as authentic was his own personal brand, which convicted the majority of men of immorality because they did not renounce their private property, because they did not work with their hands, because they ate flesh-meat and smoked tobacco. But he was not strong enough to realize moral maximization for himself; love became for him a law without grace, a source of indictment. Tolstoy had a well-balanced critical faculty, he could diagnose sin and describe well the unchristian character of his contemporary society and culture; but he did not see Christianity itself, hidden behind the sinfulness, imperfections, and deformities of Christians. Pride in his own reason prevented him from becoming interiorly Christian, Christ remained an external teacher and could not be welcomed within. But Tolstoy was a man of genius, great in his search for divine truth. Many men who have neither his genius nor his thirst for truth attack both Christianity and Christians without trying to realize any perfection in their own existence and without the problem of the meaning and justification of life causing them any suffering, much or little.

VI

It is a mistake to suppose that it is easy to live according to our Lord's commands, and to condemn his teaching because Christians do not practise it. But it is also a mistake to suppose that there is no need to realize the fulness of Christianity in the whole of life. At every moment of his existence the Christian ought to seek a perfection like to that of his heavenly Father and to lay claim to the divine Kingdom; all his life is subject to the words "Seek ye first the kingdom of God and his justice, and all these things shall be added unto you." The fact that our nature is sinful and that the ideal is in every way unattainable on earth must not paralyse our striving after perfection or quench our longing for the kingdom and righteousness of God. Man has to try to apply divine truth without worrying about how it will be realized in the fulness of life. The truth of Christ must be so realized, though little may be accomplished on earth, though a man may give but an hour of his life to it; and the right way is found in the effort to fulfil it and to find the heavenly kingdom without criticizing our neighbour.

Christianity is entering upon an entirely new era. Henceforth it will be impossible to live the faith only exteriorly, to stop short at a ceremonial devotion; believers will have to take the full actualization of their religion more seriously, they will have to defend it by their own personalities, by their lives, by their faithfulness to Christ and his principles, by meeting hatred with love.

In the Orthodox Church to-day the better elements, those most sincere and enthusiastic, most capable of self-sacrifice and faithfulness to our Lord, are coming to the front, while she is being abandoned by those who were Orthodox only outwardly or from habit, without understanding of their faith and what it committed them to. It may be said that the age of a confused Christianity and paganism is at an end and that a new and better one has begun. Christianity had become a dominating, an established, State religion, and the Church was tempted by the sword of Cæsar: she even used it against those whose faith was not in agreeemnt with that of the orthodox rulers. It was for this reason, because Christianity had become associated with the idea of persecutor rather than that of persecuted, that the conscience of many judged it to have ceased to be the religion of the Cross; it was too often interpreted as a sanctification of heathen customs that did not call for any real illumination and transfiguration. The time has now come when Christianity is persecuted anew, and a greater heroism, a greater expiatory love, a more complete and conscientious confession of the faith are asked for from Christians. We shall no longer be a stone of offence in the path of our religion.

VII

The Christian faith tells us to seek first the kingdom of God and divine perfection, but it will have nothing to do with day-dreaming, utopias, or false imagination: it is realist, and the Fathers of the Church are always appealing for spiritual sobriety. Christian consciousness has a clear perception of all the difficulties that beset the way of perfection, but it knows that "the kingdom of Heaven suffereth violence and the violent take it by force." Christianity teaches us to work from within to the outward and not *vice versa;* the perfect life, whether individual or social, cannot be attained through any programme imposed externally: spiritual rebirth is essential and it proceeds from freedom and grace. Compulsion will never make good Christians or a Christian social order; there must be an effective and real change in the hearts of persons and of peoples, and the realization of this perfect life is a task of infinite difficulty and endless duration.

The negation of Christianity due to the shortcomings of Christians is essentially the ignoring and misunderstanding of original sin. Those who are conscious of original sin see in the unworthiness of Christians not a flat contradiction of the worth of Christianity but a confirmation of it. It is the religion of redemption and salvation, and is not forgetful that the world finds pleasure in sin. There are many teachers who claim that the good life can be compassed without any real overcoming of evil, but Christianity does not think so: it insists on this victory, a rebirth; it is radical and more exacting.

Many men and things in history were decked out with Christian emblems that they did not deserve. There is nothing baser than lies, simulation, and hypocrisy, and this state of things provoked protest and revolt. The State bore the name and symbols of Christianity without being effectively Christian, and the same could be said of everything else, science, art, economics, law, the whole of "Christian culture." There were even those who tried to uphold the rich and great of this world and the social exploitation of man by man by an appeal to Christianity! The heathen man still lived on in Christendom; he was called to take his part in the building up of Christian life but meanwhile the old evil passions continued to stir within him: the Church influenced him interiorly but she could not alter his nature by force—the process had to be inward and hidden, God's kingdom comes imperceptibly. A vast amount of hypocrisy, falsehood, convention, and empty rhetoric accumulated in Christendom, and insurrection against it was inevitable. The revolt against and rejection of Christianity often represented simply a sincere wish for the outside to be like the inside: if there is no interior religion then there should be none exterior, if the State and society and culture are not Christian then they should not be called so; there is no need to sham and tell lies. Such a protest has its positive side in hatred of falsehood and love of truth; but along with its truth and sincerity, its protest against lies and hypocrisy, there went a new lie and a new hypocrisy.

Starting from the premise that men and society were in fact only imitation Christian the stage was reached where it was affirmed that Christianity itself is untrue and a myth, that the failure of men means the exploding of their religion. The critics then began to flatter themselves that they had reached a higher level, a greater perfection, a more authentic profession of faith. Thus anti-Christian hypocrisy took the place of Christian hypocrisy, and the adversaries of Christianity esteemed themselves, as such, more virtuous and enlightened and understanding of truth than mere Christians can be. Actually, these people were led astray by the worldly view which denies truth because it is more impressed by its perversions than by its reality. In that they have lost the sense of sin they are inferior to Christians. Nietzsche fought Christianity passionately because he looked only at degenerate and outward Christians; as for the Christian religion, he never began to try to understand it.

The Christian world is undergoing a crisis which is shaking it to its foundations. The day of sham, outward, rhetorical religion is past and henceforward it will be impossible to wed the externals of Christianity with a deceitful paganism. An age of effective realism is beginning which is tearing away the veils that hide the primordial realities and bringing the human soul face to face with the mysteries of life and death. Social conventions, political and governmental forms have lost all significance; men want to penetrate to the depths of life, to learn what is essential and what useful, to live in truth and righteousness.

Under the influence of contemporary upheavals souls are born thirsting above all for an unobscured and undeformed truth. Man is tired of falsehood and conventions and all the forms and appearances that have taken the place of reality; he wants to see the truth of Christianity, shorn of the deceptions which bad Christians have imposed on it; he wants to come to Christ himself. The Christian renaissance will be above all an appeal to Christ and to his truth freed from all human perversion and adaptation. Man's renewed consciousness of the permanent fact of original sin need not weaken consciousness of his responsibility towards the work of our Lord in the world or nullify endeavours for the forwarding of that work. To make the truth and commands of Christ real sometimes seems a desperate, impossible undertaking, and Christianity itself tells us that it is a task that cannot be achieved by our unaided human powers. But what is impossible for man is possible for God. He who believes in Christ knows that he is not alone: he knows that he is called to realize the truth of Christ in company with Christ himself, his saviour.